Published by Sabree Publications
P.O. Box 1301
Orange, New Jersey 07051

(A Division of Sabree Communications Inc.)

Copyright C 1995 by Amin bin Qasim Nathari

ISBN 1-887513-00-0

All Rights Reserved. No portion of this book may be reproduced without written permission from the author.

First Printing - June 1995

CONTENTS

Acknowledgements

Introduction 1

Preface: Reflections 11

Chapter 1   The Nation of Islam
1930 - 1975: A Brief History 17

Chapter 2   February 25, 1975:
The Death of Elijah Muhammad 57

Chapter 3   "I Was Born For The Mission": Wallace D. Muhammad assumes the leadership of the Nation of Islam 66

Chapter 4   From Wallace D. Muhammad to W. Deen Mohammed: An Analytical Critique of his Leadership and Teachings 78

Chapter 5   Breaking Away: Louis Farrakhan Goes Solo 132

Chapter 6   Minister Louis Farrakhan and the 'new and revived' Nation of Islam 142

Chapter 7   The Islamic View of Elijah Muhammad and the Nation of Islam: Judging in Light of the Quran and the authentic Sunnah of the Messenger of Allaah (SAAWS).................164

Chapter 8   "Muslim American Spokesman for Human Salvation": The Ministry of Imam W. Deen Mohammed; A Close Examination...........182

Chapter 9   A Refutation of All Blind Following: Refer It Back to Allaah and His Messenger !!! (SAAWS).......................198

Chapter 10   Where Do We Go From Here? A Brief Look at the Current State of the Muslim Ummah in America 209

Summary and Closing Thoughts..............223

Bibliography 230

Selected Reading List...............................234

About the Author.......................................237

ACKNOWLEDGMENTS

Verily all praise, gratitude and credit belongs to Allaah, The Most High. It is related that Allaah's Messenger, our Prophet Muhammad, salla allaahu alahi was salaam (may Allaah's peace be upon him) said in an authentic narration:

"WHOEVER DOES NOT THANK ALLAAH DOES NOT THANK THE PEOPLE, AND WHOEVER DOES NOT THANK THE PEOPLE DOES NOT THANK ALLAAH. "

With that, after thanking Allaah, I would like to thank my family; my parents Abu Amin Qasim and Wafiyyah Nathari for their support and encouragement throughout this project (and throughout my entire life!); my wife Lisa, whose editing, as well as her input and concern for this work was very instrumental in this project; my sister Taminah, especially for her assistance in developing the mailing list and my son Amir ibn Amin for always patiently understanding when "Abu has to work".

I love you and may Allaah protect and preserve all of you.

I also have to thank three of my dear brothers in Islam, and comrades in this dawah for the struggle against ignorance in our religion and way of life; Mujahid Abdur-Rahman from the Center for Dawah Initiatives, who has helped to open the way for me to have many opportunities to spread this important message. His support and encouragement has been very important to me. It is a pleasure and truly a blessing from Allaah to be able to work and travel with a brother who has such a sincere concern and commitment to the Muslims and this dawah.

Abu Tasneen Dawud Adib, for his comments and assistance in " Islamic editing" this work and his efforts to help in providing an Arabic translation for this work so that many others can be informed and benefit from this project; and Abu Usamah Khalifah at-Thahabi, for his sincere naseeha (advice) and for helping me to ensure that every single hadith (narration) from Allaah's Messenger (SAAWS) was authentic. May Allaah protect and preserve all of these brothers and their families.

Allaah knows best, it would take an entire chapter to thank all of those, (family, associates, etc.) who have supported, encouraged and assisted in this project. So as not to neglect mentioning anyone, I ask that Allaah reward all of the Muslims who encouraged, helped and supported this work (and those who didn't) with much good.

I also thank the non-Muslims who have expressed their support for this book, and through their questions in my conversations with them, reaffirmed the need for such a book. I ask Allaah to allow them to become enlightened and benefit from the information in this work, and that He guide them, as well as the other non-Muslims who assisted in the various aspects (production, printing, technical, etc.) of this project to accept this truth, the best way of life, the religion with Allaah; Al-Islam.

ISLAM IN AMERICA 1995

INTRODUCTION

Verily all praise is for Allaah. We praise Him, seek His help and ask for His forgiveness. We seek refuge in Allaah from the evil within ourselves and from our evil actions. Whomsoever Allaah guides, none can misguide and whomsoever Allaah misguides, none can guide. I bear witness that none has the right to be worshipped except Allaah, alone, having no partner and I bear witness that Muhammad is His Servant and Messenger.

O you who believe! Fear Allaah as He should be feared and die not except as Muslims.

O mankind! Be dutiful to your Lord, Who created you from a single person (Aadam) and from him, He created his wife (Eve) and from them both He created many men and women; and fear Allaah through Whom you demand your mutual (rights) and do not sever the family ties. Surely, Allaah is ever an All-Watcher over you.

O you who believe! Keep your duty to Allaah and fear Him, and speak

20 YEARS A.E. (after Elijah)

(**always**) the Truth. He will direct you to do righteous deeds and will forgive you your sins. Whosoever obeys Allaah and His Messenger has indeed attained a great achievement.

As for what follows: Surely the best speech is the book of Allaah and the best guidance is the guidance of His Messenger; And the worst of all affairs in this deen are newly invented matters, for every newly invented matter is an innovation; every innovation is an astray; and every astray is in the Hell-Fire.

I begin by asking Allaah to guide us and make my intention pure and solely for His acceptance. I also ask Allaah to allow the reader to have an open mind, a clear heart and accept whatever words of truth that are contained in these words.

We live in a land, North America, specifically the United States of America, that is full of misguidance and corruption in various aspects. Unfortunately, the aforementioned illnesses and imperfections have found their way into the correct understanding and practice of our way of life as Muslims, Al- Islam.

ISLAM IN AMERICA 1995

This misguidance and corruption has manifested itself in many forms. The most major of them being deviance; meaning deviance from the guidance of the book of Allaah, the Quran and the methodology of Allaah's Messenger, our Prophet Muhammad, salla allaahu alahi was salaam (Allaah's peace be upon him). Deviance by words, interpretation and implementation.

There are many groups, sects, and organizations all happily rejoicing in their own programs and agendas, all the while falsely waving the banner of Islam. Amongst these groups which are many, some are more prominent than others. Some are clearly far astray, while others are on the verge but still within the fold of Islam.

We also have many groups and organizations that have done a lot of good and have always strived their best to uphold Islam and implement the methodology of Allaah's Messenger (SAAWS) to the best of their ability. Many of these groups were in existence prior to 1975! Allaah has promised that there will always be present those among the people that will defend this deen.

20 YEARS A.E. (after Elijah)

Inshallah, (Allaah willing), in our next project, Islam and the Muslims in America.....Then and Now, we will pay closer attention to examining these groups, their works, and the stories of many who then and now worked in the cause of establishing Islam in America even when the masses of people were astray.

This book is not an effort to bash any particular person, group or organization, etc. It is simply an effort to examine these groups and individuals and their claims of Islam and assess them using the best criteria, the Quran and the authentic Sunnah of Prophet Muhammad (SAAWS). In doing this we consequently reject and refute the deviant, misguided and the astray groups and their leaders, as we have been commanded to do. Allaah's Messenger (SAAWS) said in an authentic narration (translated):

"WHOEVER INTRODUCES OR INVENTS SOMETHING INTO THIS AFFAIR OF OURS (RELIGION) AND IT IS NOT OF IT, HE WILL HAVE IT REJECTED!"

So I feel that it is obligatory for me to

ISLAM IN AMERICA 1995

write this book and to be as honest and forthcoming as possible, for we are commanded by Allaah to speak a word of truth even if it be against our own selves! So if you read anything in these words that may seem to be against your leader, Imam, Shaikh, etc., remember this simple rule: In Islam, no one is above the law!

The Quran and the authentic Sunnah is the unquestionable, unadulterated and absolute authority for the Muslim. Anything else or anyone else that does not measure up to these standards is subject to scrutiny and again, will be rejected. Don't look at it as someone `dissing' your Imam or Shaikh, accept it for what it is; defending Allaah, His Messenger (SAAWS) and this deen!

This book, Islam in America: 1995, 20 Years A.E. (after Elijah) will focus primarily on a period of twenty (20) years, the past 20 years from 1975 to 1995. I think that most observers will agree and surely Allaah knows best, that this period of time over the last 20 years has been the most important and critical time for Islam and the Muslims in this country. As the book will make increasingly clear, this year

20 YEARS A.E. (after Elijah)

1995 is certainly a time for reflection and self examination.

For many of us, myself included, 1975 began a period of evolution, from darkness and ignorance into light. And this process is still continuing. This book will cover in detail just how far we have come, and how far many of us still have to go. I think that now is the time to do a fair analysis of the past 20 years of history of Islam in America, both Islam as defined by the Quran and the Sunnah and "Islam" as many of us thought it was in ignorance.

Unfortunately, many of us still want to see things for what we wish they were or could be instead of as they really are. May Allaah guide all of us who are really sincere seekers of the truth.

Finally, as we begin the journey, I humbly ask that you honor this request: Read this book for yourself. Don't rely on someone else to summarize their perception and opinion of this book. Before making a judgment or assessment of this book, read it completely, then read it again. Lastly, judge the book historically,

ISLAM IN AMERICA 1995

scholastically, unemotionally, and factually. And above all judge what I write by the Quran and Sunnah and judge anyone or anything refuted or scrutinized in this book by that same criteria, the Quran and the authentic Sunnah.

And if you should find anything of a factual nature that is incorrect, please contact me in writing. Inshallah, (Allaah willing) I am in the process of researching and writing a much needed and extensive fact filled history book. In this book, as I stated earlier, we will focus on the total picture of Islam in this country covering the stories, experiences and works of many groups and individuals. Anything that is thought and proven to be factually incorrect can be addressed in this future work.

You will also notice that throughout this book I stress the authentic Sunnah of Allaah's Messenger (SAAWS). I can not emphasize enough the importance of our understanding the authentic Sunnah. Especially since we have those among us (may Allaah guide them) that consistently minimize and even negate the importance and role of the

20 YEARS A.E. (after Elijah)

Sunnah of Allaah's Messenger (SAAWS).

They even minimize the status of Allaah's Messenger (SAAWS)! They refer to him casually as "Muhammad, The Prophet of Arabia", "The Prophet", etc. Often times they don't even send salutations on our Prophet (SAAWS)! It is well known by Muslims that Allaah curses the one who doesn't send salutations on His Messenger (SAAWS)! They talk about the Messenger of Allaah (SAAWS) as if he was just some regular person that we pass everyday on the streets, in the masjid, etc. As you will see throughout this book, this is THE main reason for the condition that we are in today, in 1995!

What is even more disturbing is the influential or so-called "knowledgeable" people in some of these groups even go so far as to constantly lie on Allaah's Messenger (SAAWS) by using weak, even forged hadiths, saying that he said things that he never said!!! This even after they have been shown the clear way and the majority of the Muslims all over the world know that these "hadith" are fabricated fairy tales.

I won't mention any of these stories here, as in later chapters we will highlight some of them. But many of us know them and have heard them all. For now, I will say this: Allaah's Messenger (SAAWS) has said in an authentic narration:

WHOEVER LIES ON ME AND SAYS THAT I SAID SOMETHING THAT I DID NOT SAY, LET HIM TAKE HIS SEAT IN THE HELLFIRE!!!

We seek refuge with Allaah from such ignorance and misguidance.

People give more respect and reverence to their Shaikhs and Imams, living and dead. A person will say, with great love and reverence, "The Honorable Elijah Muhammad" and then very casually say "Prophet Muhammad of Arabia" in the same sentence! It is obvious that we still have a long, long way to go towards understanding this deen, Al-Islam, as revealed by Allaah in the Quran to our Prophet Muhammad (SAAWS), and as understood and implemented by his companions, our pious predecessors, and the generations who followed in their way.

20 YEARS A.E. (after Elijah)

I will do my best, with the help of Allaah, to put the past 20 years of Islam in America in the proper historical context, and analyze it based on what we have been given as a judge and as the best example for all of our affairs. As Allaah has said in the Quran (translated):

Surely in the Messenger of Allaah you have the best example for all of those whose hope is in Allaah and the Last Day.

Again, we ask Allaah to guide us all along the Straight Way, the way of those on whom He has granted His favor. For surely whomever Allaah has guided none can misguide. And whomever has been misguided because of some disease of the heart or due to following some ideology foreign to the truth of Islam, surely none can guide.

ISLAM IN AMERICA 1995

PREFACE : REFLECTIONS

Newark International Airport, May 9, 1994. As I look around I find myself surrounded by Muslims, men, women, adults and children, all gathered to send off a group of believers to perform the rites of Hajj. I know personally nearly everyone in the group, the brothers leaving for Saudi Arabia and the throngs of family, friends and other well wishers assembled there. Some of these brothers are like uncles and older brothers to me. But this group has an even more significant meaning to me: my father who has been like my brother, my mentor and confidant all my life is part of this group.

Alhamdulillah (praise be to Allaah), I am able to bear witness to Islam in America coming full circle in my lifetime. The pilgrimage to Mecca or Hajj is the fifth pillar of Islam. It is a journey to the sacred city of Mecca highlighted among many other things by a visit to the Kabaa', the house that prophet Ibrahim (Abraham) alahi salaam built as the first place of worship for Allaah. The Hajj should be fulfilled at least once in ones'

20 YEARS A.E. (after Elijah)

lifetime by those who can physically, financially and otherwise afford to do so.

As I hug the brothers before they board the plane and I embrace my father before he leaves me, I struggle (unsuccessfully) to hold back the tears. These tears are of various emotional origin. They are tears of happiness, of course, for those fulfilling this principle of our faith and a lifelong dream and goal of every Muslim. And they are tears of sadness, wishing that I was part of the group and asking Allaah to allow me to make this Hajj before I die.

But I find that most of all, upon further reflection and introspection, these tears are of anger, pain and overwhelming gratitude to Allaah for saving me (and many others) from total darkness and ultimate ruin! Inshallah (Allaah willing), as you read this book you will understand these emotions clearly. But as a brief introduction I sincerely share with you this:

My thoughts begin to go back to my childhood, my most clearest, most accurate memories go back to 1969,

ISLAM IN AMERICA 1995

where at age five (5) I eagerly awaited and anticipated getting on an airplane for the first time. The excitement of riding on the plane was nothing in comparison to the reason for the trip.

I would finally get to see 'live and in person' the man whom I was taught (and believed in my heart for years to follow as did many others) was THE last Messenger of Allaah! audhu billah (I seek refuge with Allaah). A messenger sent to the black man and woman of America. I would finally get to see the "Honorable" Elijah Muhammad, leader and teacher of the Lost-Found "Nation of Islam". To me as a child, and to literally thousands of African-American or American black people during that time, this was Islam!

As we would later be blessed by Allaah to find out, this was not Islam at all. Not much of Elijah Muhammad and his Nation's man-made, concocted doctrine have anything remotely to do with Islam, based on the book of Allaah, the Quran and as understood and practiced by Prophet Muhammad ibn Abdullah, salla allaahu alahi was salaam, (may Allaah's peace be upon

20 YEARS A.E. (after Elijah)

him.) who was THE last Messenger of Allaah and the finality of all the prophets.

Contemplating further, my thoughts go back to the summer of 1973, where at age 9, I would accompany my father on regular Sunday trips (at least once a month, sometimes biweekly!) to see and hear Elijah Muhammad speak on "The Theology of Time" (which incidentally was at the height of his shirk and misguidance less than two years before his death in 1975).

My father was a minister for Elijah Muhammad in the "Nation of Islam" and he would later serve as a Minister, and as an Imam under Elijah Muhammad's son Wallace (now known as Imam W. Deen Muhammad) when he assumed the leadership upon his father's death in 1975.

By this time at age 9, I had developed a stronger sense of the Nation's presence and of what I thought to be Islam. As I, (like thousands of others) would later realize, I was no more than a pagan, idol worshipping black nationalist, headed for certain

ISLAM IN AMERICA 1995

destruction! It is with this realization that I sincerely share my reflections in beginning to write this book.

It also makes me remember that I am obligated and indebted to Allaah and He alone to correct many of the misconceptions, the misunderstandings and in some cases, blatant fabrication of what has happened since 1975, 20 years A.E. (after Elijah). We will use factual data derived from extensive research and from personal experience, that of myself and others who lived to see what happened then and where we are today, in 1995.

It is my sincere hope that the reader, both Muslim and non-Muslim, can gain a better understanding of what Islam really is and thus be able to accurately analyze the past 20 years of Islam and the Muslims in America.

This book will sadden some, anger others, offend some and make others happy. But above all, inshallah, it will educate and enlighten many and provide a forum for intelligent commentary, truthful discussion, and inspire a greater commitment to shed falsehood and hold on to the truth.

20 YEARS A.E. (after Elijah)

Because in the final analysis, our only commitment is to the truth.

And if I can shed some light on the truth for the reader and we all can analyze our past, present and future using the truth of Islam, then all the credit belongs to Allaah. And only the mistakes are mine.

Amin bin Qasim Nathari
May 1994
East Orange, New Jersey USA

CHAPTER ONE THE NATION OF ISLAM 1930 through 1975: A BRIEF HISTORY

The concept of groups and individuals falsely proclaiming Islam, prophethood, divinity, etc. is nothing new. This has always been a reality that existed through a number of sources. All of these groups have always been antagonistic and in clear opposition to the universal message of the last and greatest of Allaah's prophets and messengers, Muhammad ibn Abdullah (SAAWS).

This misguidance was even evident during the time of Prophet Muhammad (SAAWS) with Musailima Al-Kadhab (the Liar) who had the audacity to claim prophethood during the lifetime of our Prophet (SAAWS). Throughout time an assortment of groups, all astray from the truth, have arisen, cropped up and emerged, calling people to the left and the right of Allaah's straight path. This is in clear contradiction to the very fundamental commandments of Allaah and His Messenger (SAAWS).

20 YEARS A.E. (after Elijah)

One of the common features of all of these pseudo-Islamic groups is that every one of the leaders of these groups who claim to be prophets, messengers and divinely inspired, all profess that they were sent to serve a specific ethnic group of people. This is absolutely against Islam and Allah states in the Quran (translated):

SAY: OH HUMANITY! I AM THE MESSENGER OF ALLAAH TO YOU. ALL OF YOU!

Here, Allaah is commanding His Messenger, Prophet Muhammad (SAAWS) to say this. He is clearly showing us that not only has the Prophet (SAAWS) been sent by Allaah, but he has been sent to all of humanity, regardless of race, ethnicity, nationality, tribe, etc.

Continuing, in the nineteenth century the Hindus (with "a little help" from the British government) created the Qadianis and their false prophet, Ghulam Ahmed. This man was a major deviant, and his group and their doctrine, like many others that would follow after them, appeared in many American cities, especially in the African-American communities. In

ISLAM IN AMERICA 1995

the twentieth century, an ever increasing number of astray groups arose. They all have the same fundamental traits in common. They all claimed Islam, used and distorted some "Islamic" terminology and phrases, and they were all astray!!!

There were a number of groups, among them the Moorish Science Temples, led by a man named Timothy Drew, who later referred to himself as "The Prophet Noble Drew Ali". This group even had their own version of the Quran! They called it the "Holy Koran" and it contained the lessons and teachings of Drew and other esoteric, mystical materials.

This group was so far astray that they believed that Drew was Prophet Muhammad (SAAWS) reincarnated! (audhubillah). In any event, this was one of the first nationalist groups in 20th century America that claimed some Islamic basis. This group is still in existence today, although they are scarce and scattered. And as for the false prophet Drew, he was eventually killed.

More recently, a group calling itself the "Ansaru Allah Community"

20 YEARS A.E. (after Elijah)

emerged. It's leader, Dwight York, after changing his name to Isa Abdullah, began to invite African-American youth to a black nationalist version of Islam that he concocted.

Of course, as did those before him, he claimed to be the Mahdi, complete with divine insight, spiritual powers, etc. His doctrine was filled with the characteristic distortions of Islam, blatant lies against Allaah, His Messenger (SAAWS), the Quran, and many other atrocities.

This group ruined the lives of many innocent people and led many people astray throughout the 1970's and 80's. At last report, this group has changed it's name, altered it's doctrine and it's leader allegedly denounced Islam. This is rather ironic since what he taught and practiced was not Islam to begin with.

There were many other groups that came and went. Some are more well known and visible than others. This is due to various reasons, among them financial support, media exposure, etc. But clearly, without a doubt, the most powerful and influential organization to emerge

ISLAM IN AMERICA 1995

from the African-American community in the history of this country was the so-called "Nation of Islam."

No work documenting the history of the evolution of Islam in this country can be complete without an analysis and examination of this group. Even today, this group still has an enormous impact on how people perceive Islam and the Muslims in America.

The popular media has always given this group and its' program, beliefs, etc. more attention and focus than the growth of real, true Islam.

The first thing that I must stress from the start, and if the only understanding that one attains from this project is this point, the effort will have been successful: The Nation of Islam, under Elijah Muhammad and under Louis Farrakhan who is responsible for the "rebirth" of this group and currently claims its leadership, has absolutely nothing in common with Islam, the religion of Islam as defined by Allaah in the Quran and as understood and practiced by Prophet Muhammad

20 YEARS A.E. (after Elijah)

(SAAWS) and his companions, our rightly guided predecessors.

The only thing that Elijah Muhammad, Louis Farrakhan and the membership of the Nation of Islam have in common with the Muslims is the fact that they are human beings! That is it. Every aspect of their belief, understanding and practice was and is clearly and diametrically opposed to the very fundamental foundation of Islam.

I think that I am correct in assuming that nearly everyone has some knowledge of the history of "the Nation", as it has often been documented.

Most often it has been "documented and analyzed" by one of the following:

1. Someone who was never "in the Nation" and is analyzing it to either glorify or demonize it. This is usually done to support whatever point that they want to make or any agenda that they want to support.

2. Someone who was "in the Nation", professes to have grown and moved

away from this ideology but still has a strong emotional attachment to it. They will not view this group Islamically or totally objectively no matter how much they profess to do so. This is the category of people that we most often find today.

3. Someone who is still "in the Nation" and currently supports and expouses its' programs, beliefs, etc. Of course, the analysis from this camp will certainly be biased and totally in support of this group.

4. Someone who was "in the Nation" and now that they are no longer of this ideology, they analyze this group based on some negative experience that they may have had (mistreatment by an N.O.I. "official", etc.). Consequently, their argument is usually dismissed as "axe grinding" or "holding a grudge".

There are many other variations of the afore mentioned categories of "analysis" but we have summed them up into those four camps.

Now, my sincere attempt here in this chapter and throughout this book in

20 YEARS A.E. (after Elijah)

various places (and may Allaah help me in my efforts) is to do the following:

1. Give a brief, concise history of this group based on what has already been documented.

2. Clarify some of the previous documentation by sharing my personal experience and observations in this group. My analysis is as someone who was "in the Nation" and has NO emotional, financial or other attachment to its teachings, ideology, leader, etc.

3. To take my analysis, using this groups own ideology and beliefs (using statements from its leader, his "teachings", "lessons", etc., most of which are still available with some research and effort) and form a conclusion solely and completely based on the Quran and the authentic Sunnah of Allaah's Messenger (SAAWS), which is the foundation for Islam.

In attempting to do this we will in some cases make point by point comparisons of "the Nation" versus Islam. This should illustrate very

ISLAM IN AMERICA 1995

clearly, in plain, uncomplicated language, what ideology "the Nation" under Elijah Muhammad, the self-proclaimed "Messenger of Allaah," expoused for over forty years and what Islam and the REAL Messenger of Allaah, Prophet Muhammad ibn Abdullah (SAAWS), has said about these aspects. As Allaah has said in the Quran (translated):

"Nay, we hurl the Truth against falsehood, and it knocks its brains out and behold - falsehood perishes!" And surely Allaah's promise is true. Allaahu Akbar (Allaah is the Greatest).

Also bear in mind that since 1975 and even now, 20 years A.E., we have heard and still continue to hear all of the arguments, analogies, theories, rationalizations and every excuse ever used to defend Elijah, "the Nation", even W.D. Fard (a.k.a. Master Fard Muhammad, Wallace Dodd Ford, among other aliases). We have heard every defense of what they believed, taught and practiced.

Throughout this work, you will see some of these defenses and in each case you will see the best of proofs

20 YEARS A.E. (after Elijah)

and cross-examinations against this defense, the words of Allaah, the final judge, as contained in His book, the Quran and the words and example of His Messenger (SAAWS) that are contained in his authentic Sunnah.

A very important point needs to be made here:

This book is examining the "Nation of Islam" and assessing it as a religious movement, not as a social program or nationalist organization. For certain, we have to give the appropriate credit to the "Nation of Islam" as a social reform movement, and acknowledge it's work as having a positive impact, socially and economically.

The climate of America for oppressed people during this period, particularly for African-American people, was hostile at best and debilitating at worst. The civil rights movement was basically ineffective in it's efforts to affect a real change in the status of African-Americans. The climate was ripe for anyone calling to a sense of self-worth, self-empowerment and the overall uplift of the plight of African-Americans. Any movement that did not take the "turn the other cheek" or "we shall overcome" approach to our situation was certainly a unique and welcome change. The grassroots people in America had grown tired of the status quo.

Elijah Muhammad and the "Nation of Islam" offered hope to a people who had virtually given up. The ideology, philosophy and programs of the movement appealed to those who felt that Christianity had failed them. The main appeal for most of those who joined the movement was not the religious ideology, but the social and economic ideology. This is what set the "Nation of Islam" apart from all other movements during this time.

"Do for Self" was one of the movement's main themes, and it was central to the development of the character of the people who joined. These individuals came from a variety of backgrounds. Some were from dysfunctional families, many had been at odds with the "law of the land", some had even been in prison. Many had never known commitment and dedication to anything worthwhile. They never had anything that they could call their

20 YEARS A.E. (after Elijah)

own. The "Nation of Islam" provided all of this.

Elijah Muhammad would become the father figure that many never had and longed for. The members of the movement would be the family structure that they never experienced. The organizational structure of the movement would provide the discipline and stability that they desperately needed. Morally, socially and economically, the "Nation of Islam" was the model for the African-American community at that time.

In my conversations with many who were members of the movement, I often hear many people reflect on how their parents were not supportive of their decision to join the movement. However, after seeing the dramatic change that it had on their conduct and character, those same parents said that if the movement could get them to straighten up like this, it had to be a worthwhile or good program.

This sentiment was echoed in the African-American communities throughout America. The person who used to be the neighborhood "terror" was now clean, respectful and a beacon of light for them.

The concern, love and mutual cooperation among the common members of the movement was at a level that is still missing from some Muslim communities today. The importance of the family structure was prominent; you hardly ever saw a father without his son, a mother without her daughter, and in most cases, the family was always seen together, as a unit. The mutual respect for one another between the members, within the movement, was prominent and the respect for the woman was a central theme.

Unfortunately, I know of many cases today where Muslim women are disrespected, sometimes intimidated by men (both non-Muslims and even Muslims with an obviously deficient understanding of Islam), and the Muslim community (i.e., the men) tolerate and excuse this type of behavior and take a generally unconcerned and passive stance. In the days of "the Nation" this type of thing was unheard of!

Anyone who was in the movement,

20 YEARS A.E. (after Elijah)

imagine for a moment what would happen if someone came into the Muhammad's University (the school of the movement) and threatened or harassed one of the women teachers or students?!? This type of behavior was unthinkable and certainly would cause one to be dealt with severely!

The "Nation of Islam" under Elijah Muhammad was a social phenomenon, the likes of which has not been duplicated to this day. When discussing or documenting the history of nationalist, grassroots organizations and social movements, "the Nation" would have to rank at the top in terms of it's effectiveness and impact. This needs to be fully understood by each and everyone who reads this book.

As Muslims today, 20 years after Elijah Muhammad, we would do well to take note of certain aspects of the movement in terms of economic, social and organizational development. This may seem like a controversial statement to some of the "purists" among us, but we have to learn from this part of the history. It is sad to say, but in many cases, on an individual level, the concern, love and loyalty that existed between the common members of the "Nation" was far greater than what exists between many Muslims today, even those of us who claim to be on right guidance.

There are so many examples in the stories of our Prophet Muhammad (SAAWS) and his Companions that show us how they developed morally, economically and socially. It can not be denied that they were highly organized! It is also clear the love and loyalty that they had for one another, and how they treated each other, even when they argued or disagreed. They truly loved for their brother what they loved for themselves. They certainly did not act the way many of us do today.

Unfortunately, the most successful attempt at implementing any real structure or organization in the African-American community still to this day was the "Nation of Islam" under Elijah Muhammad. This was with the **wrong** understanding of Allaah and an **incorrect and false concept of Islam.**

Now, by the mercy of Allaah, the

20 YEARS A.E. (after Elijah)

light of Islam has come and we are developing a correct understanding of this deen, so what is our excuse? We have the Quran and the Sunnah, and in most cases, we still have not begun to do what we have to do to strengthen and improve our overall situation .

The problem with the "Nation of Islam" is when we try to give it validity and credibility as a part of Islam. This is incorrect and it gives the uninformed the false impression that there are different kinds of Islam. It makes one think that the "Nation of Islam" was a part of Islam as given to us by Allaah in the Quran and in the Sunnah of His Messenger (SAAWS).

We have an obligation to dispel the myths and clarify any misconceptions about Islam. And we have to put the "Nation of Islam" in it's proper historical and social context. Once we can achieve this, we can learn the lessons of the history of the past 20 years, and benefit from it. We can also apply those lessons to our present situation and future circumstances, inshallah (Allaah willing).

ISLAM IN AMERICA 1995

So as you begin reading this history and brief analysis of the "Nation of Islam" from its founding in 1930 until February 25, 1975, please remind yourself of this fact: If ANYONE has a problem with anything that is said against this group **in defense of Islam**, their problem is not with me. Their problem is with Allaah and His Messenger (SAAWS)! For if a person has true faith, the truth is tasteful and pleasant to them. Consequently, anyone who does not possess this faith and does not have the correct understanding of Islam and the proper system of belief, the truth is a bitter taste indeed.

May Allaah guide our hearts and grant us all understanding.

And with that, we begin the 'journey'.....

20 YEARS A.E. (after Elijah)

A NATION IS BORN IN DETROIT AND GROWS.....1930 THROUGH 1965

"Allah came to us from the Holy City of Mecca, Arabia, in 1930. He used the name of Wallace D. Fard, often signing it W.D. Fard. In the third year (1933) He signed His name 'W.F. Muhammad' which stands for Wallace Fard Muhammad. He came alone"

The above statement of clear shirk, associating partners with Allaah, (which is a major sin in Islam) is courtesy of Elijah Muhammad. This is the opening paragraph of his book entitled *The Supreme Wisdom: Solution to the so-called Negroes' Problem*, first edition printed February 26, 1957. This book outlines much of the doctrine of the "Nation of Islam" and along with "the Lessons," composed the majority of the ideology of this group. This quotation from the book was used to set the tone for the examination of the history of "the Nation" as we know it, along with some embellishment on the part of Mr. Muhammad. The relevance of this statement will become increasingly clear as you proceed through this book.

ISLAM IN AMERICA 1995

All accounts of the origin of the "Nation of Islam" are marked by a sense of mystery and intrigue. Sometime in the summer of 1930, a friendly, and by all accounts mysterious peddler appeared in the city of Detroit, Michigan in what commonly is referred to as 'the ghetto'. This man was thought to be an Arab, although some say that he may have been European. His racial and ethnic identity has never been documented.

He was welcomed in the homes of his customers, African-Americans who were eager to see the various wares, silks, clothing, etc. He claimed the things that he sold were like those worn by African people in their native lands overseas.

His customers were excited with the chance to learn of their own culture from one who had been there. In fact, he said that he was from Africa, the land of our people. This enabled the peddler to begin holding meetings from house to house throughout the community. He became well known all throughout the community as the "prophet."

20 YEARS A.E. (after Elijah)

At first, his teachings were confined primarily to things such as diet and certain kinds of foods not to eat, how to live a longer life and improve one's physical health, and stories from "the Motherland", etc. By all accounts, he was a kind, unassuming and patient person.

His primary textbook was the Bible which he used to teach the people about their true religion, which he said was the religion of the black man of Africa and Asia. He used the Bible because he said that it was the only book that the people knew. It was not the book of the "Black Nation," but carefully interpreted (by him of course), it could serve until they were introduced to the "Holy Quran."

Gradually, by all accounts, the "prophet" as he was called, began to bitterly denounce the white race. As his status grew he also increased his attacks on Christianity and the Bible. These people who came to the house meetings, being from Christian backgrounds, became overwhelmed by what they were hearing. Many of them would convert on the spot.

By this time, the house to house

format for the meetings had proved to be inadequate. There were so many people wishing to hear the "prophet" they had to rent a hall in order to accommodate the people. They named this hall the "Temple of Islam." From this humble beginning, the group officially known as "the Lost-Found Nation of Islam in the West" was born.

Again, it is not the intention of this book to be a detailed account of the history of the "Nation of Islam." But it is important that we discuss the history of this group, as there have been so many distortions and fabrications that in order to discuss what happened after 1975, we must be absolutely clear on how it all began.

An author named Erdmann D. Beynon wrote a series of articles entitled *the Voodoo Cult among Negro Migrants in Detroit*. This work was published in the respected *American Journal of Sociology* (July 1937-May 1938). In this work, the author spoke with many of Fard's first converts. This is one of the only documented sources where we get the account of someone who was there at the initial

20 YEARS A.E. (after Elijah)

stages of Fard's teachings other than Elijah Muhammad, before he became an officer in the group, and before Fard's disappearance.

One of Fard's earliest converts, Carrie Muhammad, was quoted by Beynon in this work as saying that on one occasion, the "prophet" said: "My name is W.D. Fard, and I come to you from the Holy City of Mecca. More about myself I will not tell you yet, for the time has not come. I am your brother. You have not yet seen me in my royal robes."

As mentioned earlier, there are a number of legends and great speculation about this mysterious figure. One legend has it that he was a Palestinian Arab who had organized people in London and in India before coming to America. Others say that he was a Jamaican whose father was a Syrian Muslim. Some of his early followers even believed that he was born of royal lineage from the tribe of Quraish!

Once, when questioned by Detroit police, he proclaimed he was "the Supreme Ruler of the Universe!". One must wonder if he had been taken

ISLAM IN AMERICA 1995

seriously in this claim and dealt with accordingly, (i.e., detained for observation, and possibly institutionalized) how much better off would we be now. And surely Allaah knows best.

Fard described himself to his followers as having been sent to wake up his "uncle", the Black Nation in order to expose the "blue-eyed devil". The illiterate and mostly unlearned African-Americans of that time were fascinated by his candor and fearlessness in the face of the obviously white dominated society. Initially, the contact between Fard and the people in the ghetto was informal, relaxed and casual in nature.

After the temple had been acquired, the house to house meetings were completely discontinued and a clearly defined organizational structure was formed. In less than four years, Fard had developed an organization so efficient that he began to have almost no active involvement in the movement.

He had set up the temple and wrote two manuals, *The Secret Ritual of the*

20 YEARS A.E. (after Elijah)

Nation of Islam, and *The Teaching for the Lost Found Nation of Islam in a Mathematical Way*; founded the University of Islam, an elementary and secondary school; created the Muslim Girls Training, (known as the M.G.T. and G.C.C.) which taught the young women home economics, and various etiquettes of womanhood; and he founded the Fruit of Islam (the F.O.I.), a clean cut, much feared and respected para-military unit of men who were responsible for securing and defending "the Nation".

A Minister of Islam was appointed to run the entire organization, assisted by a staff of assistant ministers. Each of these men was initially selected by Fard and trained exclusively by him. Eventually, Fard disappeared totally from public visibility.

One of the earliest officials in the movement under Fard was Elijah Muhammad. Muhammad, born Robert Poole in Sanderville, Georgia on October 7, 1897, was one of thirteen children. His father was a Baptist preacher (which perhaps explains his heavy reliance on the Bible for his "teachings"). At age 16, he left home. Ten years later, armed with a fourth grade education, he and his wife Clara moved to Detroit. He held various jobs until the Depression began in late 1929. A year or so later, he met Fard. Elijah Muhammad devoted himself to Fard and the movement.

Withstanding opposition from some of the others in the organization, he became Fard's most trusted servant. Fard chose Muhammad (whom he initially had given the name Karriem, but to acknowledge his "higher status" renamed him Muhammad) to preside over "the Nation" as Chief Minister. Elijah Muhammad was almost singlehandedly responsible for raising Fard to the status of deity and he alone perpetuated his teachings in the early years after Fard disappeared.

Fard disappeared about June 1934 shortly after Elijah Muhammad was named Chief Minister. Fard vanished as mysteriously as he arrived. Again, many legends abound concerning his disappearance, all of which are unsubstantiated. Muhammad's critics hint at the coincidence of Fard's disappearance and Elijah's rise to power.

20 YEARS A.E. (after Elijah)

Another scenario is that Fard met with foul play at the hands of some dissident followers. Even the police have been accused of having a part in his disappearance. What we do know is that Elijah Muhammad would reign as the undisputed leader until his death in 1975.

After Fard's disappearance, the movement, to which Fard had drawn anywhere from 5 to 8,000 followers began to decline in size and impact. It was at this point that forces within the movement drove Muhammad from Detroit to Chicago where he had set up Temple No. 2 on the southside. It was there that he established the Nation's headquarters and began to systematically redefine and fine tune his movement.

Fard became identified as "Allah", he was worshipped and deified; Muhammad became known as the "Prophet", like Fard had been previously, and he also began to be referred to as "the Messenger of Allah." He developed the Nation's teaching regarding prayer, fasting, marriage, etc. All of which were far out and distorted versions of the Islamic rulings and the commandments of Allaah and His Messenger (SAAWS)!

Mr. Muhammad also began to develop the Nation's financial and economic programs. Each member was expected to give a fixed percentage of their income to the movement each year, payable weekly. To the Muslim, this will appear as just what it was: a corrupt and distorted form of Zakat, one of the five pillars of Islam. The temples on a local level collected contributions regularly for a number of local and national funds. There were six known national funds or 'charities', four were designated for real estate purchases and property acquisition, public relations, new cars for 'officials' and official travel.

Another fund was an annual collection on the anniversary of Fard's birthday called the 'Saviour's Day Gift', the discretionary fund and the No. 2 Poor Treasury was for Muhammad's usage as he saw fit. In classified intelligence documents, it is alleged that Muhammad routinely referred to this account as "my checking account".

"The Nation of Islam" stabilized and

20 YEARS A.E. (after Elijah)

pretty much functioned at the same level for a number of years. It wasn't until the 1950's and the emergence of a young man just released from prison that "the Nation" would enjoy a period of unprecedented growth and progress.

Malcolm X, born Malcolm Little joined the Nation upon his release from prison. His story is well known and it would be redundant to repeat it in any detail again in this book.

It is important however to make one thing clear. Malcolm X, who was the National Representative of the Nation of Islam until 1964 when he left the movement after being suspended ninety days earlier, did not die believing as he did when he followed Elijah Muhammad. He was murdered on February 21, 1965 as El Hajj Malik El Shabazz, a Muslim. He had the courage to stop following the ways of ignorance after Allaah allowed the light of true Islam to come to him.

He didn't continue to glorify the "Nation" like many of us still do. Many of us still suffer from the disease of pride and we compound this disease with arrogance. We won't allow ourselves to accept the fact that we were duped and led astray. And we don't thank Allaah enough or give Him alone the credit for having guided us.

For certain, if we had been left alone to die upon that which we believed, we as Muslims know what our fate could have been. We would do well to look at the example of El Hajj Malik and start judging by the Quran and the Sunnah before the Quran and the Sunnah judges us!

The position of Islam is clear in this regard. In order for something to be considered and accepted as a good deed in Islam, it has to meet two basic criteria.

1. It has to be done strictly for the pleasure of Allaah subhana huwa ta ala (Highly Glorified is He).

2. It has to be done in accordance with the book of Allaah, the Quran and in accordance with the methodology of our Prophet Muhammad (SAAWS).

20 YEARS A.E. (after Elijah)

So it can and must be emphasized here that whatever good that could have possibly come from the doctrines, beliefs and practices of the "Nation of Islam" was nullified and negated because it did not meet either of the aforementioned criteria. In an examination of the facts presented thus far, it is clear that the following atrocities against Islam were committed:

1. Elijah Muhammad and the "Nation of Islam" committed the ultimate sin, the one thing that Allaah says He does not forgive: shirk, associating partners with Allaah! He not only said that Allaah came in the person of a man, Master Fard Muhammad, but he said that "Allah" had a mother and a father! I seek refuge with Allaah from such horrible and detestable atrocities.

2. Elijah Muhammad lied on Allaah's Messenger, Prophet Muhammad ibn Abdullah (SAAWS). He said that he and not Prophet Muhammad (SAAWS) was the last messenger of Allah. He even went so far as to teach in his and Fard's lessons that our Prophet Muhammad (SAAWS) was a

member of the black nation who grieved himself to death because he could not reform the devil! These two facts are major highlights of the movement which can be found in "The Lessons" of the 'Nation of Islam' mentioned earlier.

3. He corrupted and negated the institution of Zakat, as we highlighted earlier. And we have not even begun to examine his doctrines on fasting, hajj, and matters of aqeedah (belief) such as the afterlife, etc. As you will see, his "teachings" would only get worse and more in opposition to Islam as time went on.

"The Nation" continued to grow and prosper and Elijah Muhammad's teachings continued to be in clear contradiction to Islam. And during Malcolm's time in the movement, the numbers increased to an all time high. It was gaining increasing attention in the halls of higher learning and in the media. More educated and professional people began to join the movement. Malcolm could articulate the message of the self proclaimed "Messenger" better than anyone, even Mr. Muhammad

20 YEARS A.E. (after Elijah)

himself.

As the Nation of Islam entered the 10 year period following El Hajj Malik Shabazz's murder, a number of personalities and elements, (both among the leadership and within the membership) would emerge. As we will examine, the course of events over the next ten years would change the goals and direction of the movement dramatically.

ISLAM IN AMERICA 1995

"THE NATION" CONTINUES..... 1965 THROUGH 1975

The 10 year period that preceded the death of Elijah Muhammad was a very important phase that merits close examination. It was in 1965 that Elijah Muhammad wrote his first full length book. He had written smaller pamphlets prior to this, but never a book covering his teachings in any great detail.

This book was entitled *Message to the Blackman in America*. He signed this book, "by Elijah Muhammad, Messenger of Allah, Leader and Teacher to the American So-called Negro." This book contains 330 pages of his teachings and clearly details his concepts of God, the Devil, prayer, the Judgment, his economic program and many more issues.

Each and every aspect of his teachings in this book as well as in his later books, *How to Eat to Live Books 1 and 2, The Fall of America*, and his last book, *Our Saviour Has Arrived*, all have a common thread. They all are contradictory to Islam in interpretation and implementation, in

20 YEARS A.E. (after Elijah)

concept and practice.

During this time, the circulation of the Nation's newspaper, *Muhammad Speaks* began to increase dramatically. The bulk of the exposure within "the Nation" would focus primarily on two individuals, Louis Farrakhan and Muhammad Ali. I can remember that these two were synonymous with "the Nation." Farrakhan assumed the role of National Representative after El Hajj Malik Shabazz's murder. Ali became the heavyweight boxing champion of the world prior to Shabazz's murder and was a major personality within the movement.

The appeal and charisma of these two individuals enabled the movement to rebound from the loss of a popular speaker, major attraction and a dynamic presence such as Malik Shabazz. I remember that most of the bazaars and other gatherings sponsored by the movement during the late 60's and early 70's would draw crowds in the thousands. Once at a "Black Family Day" rally in 1974 on Randall's Island in New York, a crowd of over 70,000 people assembled to hear Farrakhan speak.

While Elijah Muhammad was still clearly the leader of the movement, there was a noticeable difference in the organization. His health was failing and the only time he would really address the public was once a year at the annual "Saviour's Day" event. At the same time, during the early 70's, the nucleus of the national officials developed into a more corporate like unit.

Abass Rassoull would become the National Secretary and even more emphasis was placed on the accumulation of wealth and property under his direction. A major fund raiser to purchase a plane for Mr. Muhammad was launched. It was called "Jet for Muhammad" and it attained it's goal; a private plane was purchased.

More national fund raising efforts were happening with people like nightclub singer and entertainer Joe Tex joining the movement. He and the other personalities mentioned previously would appear in all the major cities. And the membership continued to grow along with the coffers.

20 YEARS A.E. (after Elijah)

The Fruit of Islam, led by Mr. Muhammad's son in-law Raymond Sharieff, became more of a force and adopted a "by any means necessary" approach and attitude with regards to keeping the membership in order. The movement's disciplinary policy was carried out more frequently. In spite of these efforts, there were still obvious signs of a power struggle developing on many levels for control and influence within the movement.

Those among the upper echelon of the movement knew that it would only be a matter of time before Elijah Muhammad lost the battle with his chronic illness and failing health. Although the idea of him dying was inconceivable to the common follower, those in the leadership knew better and were preparing for such a reality.

By 1974, "the Nation of Islam" was the envy of most national organizations, even most major corporations! It had over 75 temples nationwide and membership estimated at between 75,000 to 100,000 people. It owned over 15,000 acres of farmland and a newspaper with a weekly circulation of 500,000 copies!

ISLAM IN AMERICA 1995

"The Nation" held major real estate holdings, houses, apartments, owned an aircraft, a fish import operation, a major supermarket with it's own national brand, a national clothing factory, restaurants, bakeries and many other thriving and very profitable enterprises. On paper at least the movement's economic program was a success.

On the local level, there were members putting up businesses all over the country. And the criminal element would continue to grow throughout the movement. This was particularly so in the major cities like Newark, Philadelphia, Los Angeles, etc. So many misguided people ruined their lives! They were robbing banks, post offices, doing all sorts of things all under the banner of "building a nation". Many people died and some are still imprisoned and will probably remain so for the remainder of their lives.

People were severely beaten and even killed for simply challenging Elijah Muhammad or questioning his false claims of Islam, divinity, etc. Many of these people were actually practicing Muslims! A tragic example of this

20 YEARS A.E. (after Elijah)

type of mentality is a situation that occurred in Washington, DC in 1973.

Hamaas Abdul Khaalis, formerly known as Ernest T. 2X McGhee, a former national secretary of the "Nation of Islam" sent a letter to Elijah Muhammad, Louis Farrakhan and every minister of a major temple. In this letter Abdul Khaalis denounced Elijah Muhammad as a liar, called Fard Muhammad a fake and declared that "the Nation" was not a Muslim group practicing Islam as defined in the Quran.

On January 18, 1973, an eight man hit squad of members of the Philadelphia temple went to Washington, D.C. seeking revenge. They gained entry into Abdul Khaalis's home. He was away and his wife was out shopping. The hit squad proceeded to kill, in cold blood and without provocation, members of his family and friends, Muslims, who were present, including several small children. They even drowned three infants in the bathtub!

This was just one of many such incidents where people who went against the "Nation of Islam" or who

ISLAM IN AMERICA 1995

said anything about Elijah Muhammad were assaulted and in some cases lost their lives. It was common practice for such people to be publicly referred to as "hypocrites". People like Louis Farrakhan would regularly go on national radio and make threats against "hypocrites, traitors and disbelievers!" as he would label them. And again, many people believing that they were on `right guidance' would defend this falsehood without hesitation or regard for life. Theirs or anyone elses!

And we have to remember these very important facts:

Many people, maybe thousands during Mr. Muhammad's more than 40 years of leadership, died believing that what he and "the Nation of Islam" taught was Islam, in concept, belief, interpretation and practice. They died believing that Allaah "came in the person of Master Fard Muhammad" and that Elijah Muhammad was "the last Messenger of Allaah"!

And as of February 1975, the official position of Elijah Muhammad and "the Lost-Found Nation of Islam in

20 YEARS A.E. (after Elijah)

the West" was the same as it ever was, from 1930 through 1975. Forget about what we hear now about how he was "evolving", and how he was "preparing us for the change"! Shirk is shirk. Deviance is deviance. And never shall truth and falsehood be equal! And Allaah knows best!!!

I ask Allaah to forgive me for any and all the atrocities against His deen, Islam, that I committed in error, during the time of 20th century jahiliyah, popularly known as "the Nation of Islam", under the preachings and misguidance of Elijah Muhammad.

I ask this for myself and for all those innocent victims that are still living today who are in search of truth, Islam as given to us by Allaah in His book, the Quran, and as understood by His Prophet, the REAL last Messenger of Allaah, Muhammad ibn Abdullah, salla allahu alahi was salam, may Allaah's peace be upon him, his companions, family and all of those who are members of his `nation', the best nation, until the last day. Ameen

CHAPTER TWO FEBRUARY 25, 1975.....THE DEATH OF ELIJAH MUHAMMAD

My memories of this day are as clear as if it happened yesterday. I was home this particular day, because as a student of "Muhammad's University of Islam", school was closed for the "Saviour's Day" break. In the "Nation of Islam", February 26th of each and every year was considered a holiday. This is the day that "Master Fard Muhammad" was allegedly born. Members of the Nation from all over the country would make a `pilgrimage' to Chicago to see and hear Elijah Muhammad speak.

The poorest of the people would even make provisions to go. I know of a few cases where people tried to walk to Chicago from Newark! Allaah is my witness! People would not pay their rent or fulfill their other responsibilities in order to make this trip. It was considered a great honor to be able to travel to Chicago, which was "the National Headquarters". To be in Chicago for "Saviour's Day" was revered and treasured; this was like a Muslim today who is blessed to

20 YEARS A.E. (after Elijah)

perform the Hajj. This description is not an exaggeration of the ignorance of that time.

This particular year I did not travel with my parents to "Saviour's Day". I stayed at home in East Orange, New Jersey with my younger sister and a woman from "the Nation" who attended the temple that my father was the minister over. A news bulletin appeared on the television and I heard the reporter say something that I could never dream would be true: "Elijah Muhammad, leader of the Black Muslims has died at the age of 77."

Of course, my immediate response was silence. I just sort of blocked this notion out of my mind. Then as the story was being repeated over various other television networks, the telephone at our home began to ring continuously. Members of the Nation were calling each other all over the place in an attempt to make some sense of this story. Most of the people from our temple were calling to find out from the sister who was watching us if she or I had heard from my father who was already in Chicago.

ISLAM IN AMERICA 1995

It was about three (3) weeks away from my eleventh (11th) birthday, and I remember my response word for word: "The Honorable Elijah Muhammad cannot be dead! This is just some more of the devil's propaganda. He's always trying to divide our people!" I then assured the people that I knew that my father would be calling soon and that he would confirm the truth for us that Elijah Muhammad was not dead and that everything was alright.

As I mentioned earlier, my father was the minister of the temple in Elizabeth, New Jersey. He began as an assistant minister under the late James Shabazz who was the minister of Temple No. 25 in Newark, NJ. Shabazz, who was a very influential minister in "the Nation" under Elijah Muhammad, was murdered on September 4, 1973 (In an upcoming project, we will discuss James Shabazz in detail in our chapters covering the history of the "Nation of Islam" in Newark, NJ).

I remember my father's recollection of this day, February 25, 1975. In the past we've discussed it on several occasions. He said that he was in his

20 YEARS A.E. (after Elijah)

hotel room that day in Chicago and he received a telephone call from the brother who was the Fruit of Islam captain of the Elizabeth temple, Captain Joseph (now known as Yusuf Sultan Muhammad, alhamdulillah, a practicing Muslim).

He was calling from "the Nation's" restaurant, the Salaam, where a number of people, N.O.I. officials, etc. had gathered. The captain informed my father that the "Honorable Elijah Muhammad" was dead. When my father asked who gave him this information, he replied "the National Secretary". My father's response was: "Brother, he's a hypocrite! You stay right there, I'm on my way down there!"

Upon arriving at the restaurant my father said that it had been confirmed that Elijah Muhammad was in fact dead. He also was told that there would be a meeting that evening at Temple No. 2 for all ministers, captains, and secretaries. (This was the nucleus of the organizational structure of a temple). So he returned to his hotel in order to prepare for that evening's meeting and to call home with the news.

ISLAM IN AMERICA 1995

When my father called me later that day, he told me what I heard was true. He told me that Elijah Muhammad had died and that their would be a new leader who would lead "the Nation". He said that I should prepare to go to "Saviour's Day" tomorrow and try to stay strong. Hearing his voice that day gave me a lot of reassurance and I was able to rest that night after the day's 'tragic' turn of events.

Now, please carefully read these words. On the day that Elijah Muhammad died, there was a meeting that night at the "National Headquarters". This meeting was attended by all of the national officials, many who we've mentioned previously; Louis Farrakhan, Abass Rassoull, etc. It was at this meeting that Wallace D. Muhammad was formally presented to the temple officials from across the country as the new leader of the "Nation of Islam".

Now, as proof of the depth to which a deviant will sink and how this particular deviant group continually lied on Allaah without hesitation, observe what happened:

20 YEARS A.E. (after Elijah)

Abass Rassoull who was the National Secretary of the "Nation of Islam" had the audacity to say in front of this packed meeting, (in the presence of the new leader Wallace D. Muhammad), in a tone of mystique, as if his statement was so profound, he looked around as if to see who was there, leaned forward and said: **"I want you to know that our leader (Wallace D Muhammad) has met with Allah personally on at least two different occasions!"**

I've mentioned this because I want everyone to realize the nature of the ideology of this movement and to understand the mentality of the people who commit such acts. There is no level to which they won't go to continue to control and manipulate the minds of people and lead them astray. There is no understanding of Islam that can ever come from a movement like this.

We cannot accept that it is because of this group and it's leader that we are Muslims today. This alone is a statement of disbelief and misguidance because only Allaah has made us Muslims. It is in spite of this movement that many of us who were

ISLAM IN AMERICA 1995

in the "Nation" are Muslims today.

It is my opinion that February 25, 1975, the day Elijah Muhammad died, we were given an enormous opportunity. We had the chance to shut the door on the "Nation of Islam" for good! We had the ability to put Elijah Muhammad, Fard, and the "Nation of Islam" in it's proper perspective, Islamically. Allaah knows best, but I feel that the failure to stand firm on the truth from the beginning of this `transition' (as it is still referred to today, 20 years later!) is one of the major reasons for the present state of disunity among the Muslims in America.

As we close this chapter, I am providing the official statement issued by the "Nation of Islam" upon the death of Elijah Muhammad. For your reference, this statement is totally unedited and exactly as printed in the March 14, 1975 issue of *Muhammad Speaks* newspaper. It read as follows:

"The Nation of Islam issued the following statement, Tuesday Feb. 25, 1975 at 4:30 p.m. central daylight time:

20 YEARS A.E. (after Elijah)

The Muslims are heavy hearted because of the absence of our Leader, the most Honorable Elijah Muhammad. We offer these words of encouragement to His followers everywhere:

The Messenger taught us, we have five senses, but that no one sense can satisfy all the needs of the body. We should use all the senses working together. Now is the time the body must use all the senses and stay together.

The Messenger spent all His life in efforts to better the conditions of the Black man. We should try to see that we keep His principles and ideals in us. The loss of the Messenger's presence is a great loss. He worked for the unity of the Black man. It is a greater loss to lose His principles.

The Holy Qur'an teaches that we should not refer to the righteous as being dead.

The Messenger has returned to Allah. He lives on in His works, and more important, He lives on in us. His leadership remains."

ISLAM IN AMERICA 1995

Need I say more! We ask Allaah to give us the courage and conviction that He gave the companions of His Messenger, Prophet Muhammad (SAAWS) to speak against those who lie on Allaah, His Book, the Quran, His Last Messenger and defame His religion, Al-Islam.

We ask Allaah to continue our journey on His straight way, and that He exalt His REAL Messenger, Prophet Muhammad (SAAWS), his companions and all those who follow his guidance until the last day.

And may Allaah give Elijah Muhammad whatever he deserves.

We ask this of Him, we repent to Him and we ask Him to forgive us. Ameen.

20 YEARS A.E. (after Elijah)

CHAPTER THREE "I WAS BORN FOR THE MISSION": WALLACE D. MUHAMMAD ASSUMES THE LEADERSHIP OF THE NATION OF ISLAM.

We begin with the following statement reprinted and unedited from *Muhammad Speaks* newspaper March 14, 1975.

"Shrine for Messenger's remains"

Chicago - The casket with the remains of the Honorable Elijah Muhammad, the Last Messenger of Allah - May the Peace and Blessing of Allah forever be upon Him - is now at rest at Muhammad's Holy Temple of Islam, No. 2, and will remain so until a Memorial Mausoleum can be built for His permanent enshrinement.

The remains of the Messenger had originally been placed in the Mt. Glenwood Cemetery in Thornton, Ill., next to that of His wife, the late Sister Clara Muhammad pending the granting of a permit by the City of Chicago for entombment at Temple No. 2.

ISLAM IN AMERICA 1995

The casket of the Messenger of Allah has been brought to rest in a private room at Temple No. 2, and will be available for viewing in the near future."

This statement clearly illustrates the climate that existed in the "Nation of Islam" when Wallace D. Muhammad assumed the leadership. Wallace D. Muhammad, now known as W. Deen Mohammed, is one of the son's born to Elijah and Clara Muhammad. He was chosen to succeed his father and was initially referred to as "The Honorable Wallace D. Muhammad, Supreme Minister of the Nation of Islam."

On February 26, 1975, I was in Jersey City, N.J. with over 3,000 other members of the "Nation of Islam". We watched the "Saviour's Day" proceedings via closed circuit television at a movie theater that was rented out for the day. Members from all over the East Coast were in attendance that day. The mood was particularly somber on this occasion because everyone realized that Elijah Muhammad had died the day before. Remember, this was a person who we believed would live forever and that he would lead us until the return of

20 YEARS A.E. (after Elijah)

Fard.

There was a feeling of uneasiness and doubt that day. The future of "our Nation" was at stake, and many rumors were floating around. Where was "the Nation" headed? Who would be the leader? Minister Louis Farrakhan, the National representative? Minister Yusuf Shah of Temple No. 2 who was a personal assistant to Elijah Muhammad? Many possibilities were mentioned. To begin the program, there was a mini-documentary film that highlighted the life and `good works' of Elijah Muhammad. This was sort of a tribute film.

Throughout the film, which lasted two full hours, you could hear the sobs throughout the theater. People were visibly grieving, some uncontrollably. I cried like never before, but in my heart I believed that Allah (as I understood him then) had a plan and that "our people" would be alright.

To be honest, in my heart, I believed at that time that Minister Farrakhan was the logical choice to become the new leader. Of course, I felt that no

ISLAM IN AMERICA 1995

one could ever succeed Elijah Muhammad, but I also believed that out of all the ministers and personalities in "the Nation", no one had the charisma, was as articulate and could represent the movement better than Farrakhan.

As the National Representative for the past 10 years, he certainly had major visibility. He was on television, he was on the radio throughout the country and he had the good fortune of being based in the media capital of this country, New York City.

My father had always spoke highly of Farrakhan and they enjoyed a very close relationship. I had also met him and he seemed confident, personable and dynamic. A natural leader I thought. My father would later tell me that it was pretty well known within the higher circles of "the Nation" that if anything would happen to Elijah Muhammad, his son would assume the leadership. In 1974, he had become more visible again and was "teaching" in various places.

In any event, I watched and listened as the National Secretary, Abass

20 YEARS A.E. (after Elijah)

Rassoull declared before a packed house of over 20,000 people at the Chicago Amphitheater and to thousands of others watching on closed circuit television across the country, that the mantle of leadership of "the Nation" has fallen to Minister Wallace D. Muhammad.

Read his exact words, (again this was in the presence of Wallace D. Muhammad): "Today we would like to inform the world that there is no leadership crisis in the Nation of Islam. Almighty Allah, in the person of Master Fard Muhammad, the Honorable Elijah Muhammad and the Royal family have chosen Wallace D. Muhammad to lead the Nation of Islam.

I remember clearly that my initial response was one of hesitation and unfamiliarity. I had to think hard for a moment to remember that I had heard of him before. I recalled that he had been in some trouble and had been excommunicated on a number of occasions.

I also remembered that he was one of Elijah Muhammad's sons; in fact, he and his younger brother Akbar had both been mentioned at various times as "rebels". Akbar was even referred to on one occasion by his father as a "hypocrite". This was presumably because he went against his father's teachings. (He had enough courage a long time ago to say that his father's teachings were false and in most cases diametrically opposed to Islam.)

One by one, I watched all of the national officials and other N.O.I. personalities come forth to express their love for Elijah Muhammad, his family who was referred to as "the Royal Family" and their support for the new leadership. They included Muhammad Ali, who at that time was still the world's heavyweight boxing champion, Raymond Sharrieff who was Elijah Muhammad's son-in-law and the Nation's Supreme Captain and many others. I remember that this seemed like an endless parade.

The ministers from some of the largest temples in the country came forward to express their total support. Minister Abdul Rahman of Temple No. 15 in Atlanta, Georgia declared in his southern accent that "He pledged the South!". (Ironically, he now follows Louis Farrakhan).

20 YEARS A.E. (after Elijah)

Minister Abdul Karriem of Temple No. 27 in Los Angeles, California, Minister Jeremiah Shabazz of Temple No. 12 in Philadelphia, Pennsylvania and many other influential ministers addressed the audience.

Then Minister Farrakhan, after emotionally and emphatically extolling the virtues of Elijah Muhammad, went on to pledge his support to the new leadership. He even went so far as to proclaim that "No one else holds the key to divinity! no one else's knowledge could even approach the shoelace of Wallace D. Muhammad!".

Finally after Min. Farrakhan completed his comments, the moment had arrived. The climax of the day's events; we would finally get to hear the new leader of the "Lost Found Nation of Islam in America", the Honorable Wallace D. Muhammad, Supreme Minister and Servant of Allah. This was his first official title.

The room became filled with chants that had become common place at "Saviour's Day" and at other N.O.I. rallies: "Long live Muhammad. Long live Muhammad".

ISLAM IN AMERICA 1995

An important point needs to be made here. Some of the things that are written from this point on in this chapter and in the following chapters may be seen as 'controversial' for some. It may be viewed as unnecessary criticism, scrutiny, etc. My job, first as a Muslim and then as a researcher/historian and writer, is to document the facts! The reader can make whatever decision that he or she wants. I pray that Allaah blesses you to make a correct decision based on the truth of His book, the Quran and the Sunnah of His Messenger (SAAWS).

But of course, I am aware that some people in their love for their leader, will go to the extreme and exhibit more love for these personalities than they do for Allaah and His Messenger (SAAWS). My hope is that by the end of this book, those people will re-examine their positions. We all have to do some self-examination in order to see if we really love Allaah, His religion and His Messenger (SAAWS).

Going back to February 26, 1975, when Wallace D. Muhammad began his speech that day, I can recall that there was absolute silence! One can

20 YEARS A.E. (after Elijah)

not imagine the total state of undivided and devoted attention that was given to the new leader as he began to speak. In Islam, we are taught that leadership is a major trust and that not only are the leaders accountable to the people, but more importantly, they are accountable to Allaah.

As I mentioned earlier, Allaah gave us the opportunity to close the door on the shirk, misguidance and deviance of the "Nation Of Islam". Allaah knows best, but if the new leader had come before the people on this day and called the people to the correct understanding of La illaha il Allaah, Muhammadur Rasullulah (nothing deserves to be worshipped as a deity except Allaah and Muhammad is the Messenger of Allaah) the people would have listened! Remember, they already believed that he was "divinely chosen", so they would have listened to anything (as we did).

And the argument is still used today that "Elijah was preparing us for the change", so what better, more fundamental way to begin a change than to introduce the basic understanding of tawheed? For certain, the people would have been better served and the new leader, Wallace D. Muhammad would have done his own soul some good. Allaah knows best.

With the stage being set for him, with all of the pledges of undying loyalty and support, extolling of his "wisdom and knowledge", etc., how did he, Wallace D. Muhammad seize the moment? How did he carry out the trust that Allaah put upon him when he accepted this responsibility, this mantle (and a great burden) of leadership?

He stood at the podium in front of thousands of people (and many more thousands worldwide via closed circuit broadcast) and he stood with Allaah as his witness and his first words to begin his lecture were: "In the name of Allah, the Beneficent, the Merciful, who manifested Himself in the person of Master Fard Muhammad".

La haula wa la quwatta illa billah! There is no power, no might except for Allaah! Then he began to give his first lecture as the leader of the "Nation of Islam". When he completed

20 YEARS A.E. (after Elijah)

his talk, the crowd roared it's approval and confirmation of him as the leader. He was lifted into the air and hoisted upon the shoulders of all of the national officials, ministers and others that were on the stage that day. **With this, the window of opportunity closed. And Allaah knows best!**

As we will discuss in the following chapter, this day, February 26, 1975 would begin what some people still refer to 20 years later as a period of 'transition'. The Prophet Muhammad (SAAWS) identified it in the best of manners as *bidaa* or innovation, which is defined as all newly invented matters or novelties in this deen. This day would be representative of what the leadership of Wallace D. Muhammad and the "Nation of Islam" would symbolize for the few years to follow.

As I reflect back to that day, a few things that he said stand out in my mind. While researching information for this book I went back to re-read the speech in it's entirety. This speech, as well as the early teachings of W.D. Muhammad were as contrary to the Quran and the understanding and practice of Allaah's Messenger, Prophet Muhammad (SAAWS) as were the teachings of Elijah Muhammad.

As we will illustrate clearly in the following chapter, it was simply a case of the same product, with new and improved flavoring and packaging.

20 YEARS A.E. (after Elijah)

CHAPTER FOUR   FROM WALLACE D. MUHAMMAD TO W. DEEN MOHAMMED.....AN ANALYTICAL CRITIQUE OF HIS EARLY LEADERSHIP AND TEACHINGS

I must admit that this chapter is the most difficult for me to write. This is due to a number of reasons and factors that I will briefly mention. There is so much information documenting the teachings of Wallace D. Muhammad (now referred to as Imam W. Deen Muhammad). In writing this book I have read, reviewed and analyzed his teachings from February 26, 1975 to the current teachings of "the ministry of Imam W. Deen Mohammed", which I will discuss in a later chapter.

Analyzing these teachings and their effect on his leadership was a tedious process and an enormous task. He has written more books, articles and pamphlets, and has presented more lectures and other presentations over the past 20 years than his father, Elijah Muhammad, did in his more than 40 years as leader of the "Nation of Islam". A complete and thorough written review of his teachings would require volumes of work. At some point in the future, it may be necessary to undertake such a project. Allaah knows best.

For the purpose of this chapter, we will take a look at some of the major aspects and highlights of Wallace D. Muhammad's teachings, concepts and positions from 1975 through the mid 1980s'. Specifically, I will examine and critique these issues as they directly relate to the correct beliefs of Islam as given to us by Allaah in the Quran and the authentic Sunnah of His Last Messenger, our Prophet Muhammad (SAAWS).

This period of time that we will pay the closest attention to is the first 10 years, from 1975 to 1985. This period really set the direction for his leadership and the people who have followed him. This period covers three formal organizations under the leadership of Wallace D. Muhammad. They are the "Nation of Islam", where his official title was "the Honorable Wallace D. Muhammad, Supreme Minister of the Nation of Islam". The second group was the "World

20 YEARS A.E. (after Elijah)

Community of Al-Islam in the West", where he was referred to as the "Chief Minister". The third group was known as the "American Muslim Mission", where he was known as Imam W. D. Muhammad.

This 10 year period is a sensitive issue with many of those among the people who strongly support Imam Mohammed today. This time period reflects the beginning of this process which we mentioned earlier and is still referred to today by many from among his community as the "transition". Anytime someone, in defense of the Quran and Sunnah, says anything that is in opposition to an opinion or position expressed by "the Imam" (as he is referred to), it is considered as an "attack on our leadership".

It can be a position that Imam Mohammed has taken concerning a point of basic aqeedah (belief) where he is clearly incorrect and contrary to the position and guidance of the Quran and Sunnah. This can be in the face of all kinds of irrefutable proofs and evidence, but it does not matter.

ISLAM IN AMERICA 1995

This misguidance and blind following reaches so far that this past Ramadan, an (Islamically) ignorant Imam went so far as to threaten another Muslim, make derogatory references about him, and use profanity when speaking about him in the Jumah khutbah (Friday prayer sermon)! Why? Because the brother dared to say something viewed as critical of "the Imam" and his community. It did not matter that based on the evidence in the Quran and the Sunnah, the brother's statement was totally correct! May Allaah guide us and cure us of the diseases of ignorance and arrogance.

All of these things happen simply because we have not yet developed an understanding of what Islam really is and what it really means when we say we are Muslims. And for sure, we certainly have not fully comprehended that the best speech is the book of Allaah, the Quran, and the best guidance is the guidance of the Prophet Muhammad (SAAWS).

Imam Malik, rahimuhullah (may Allaah have mercy on him), was one of the knowledgeable, studious and sincere Imams of our great past, and

20 YEARS A.E. (after Elijah)

a REAL scholar. One day he was sitting with a group of people in the Prophet's Masjid. He emphatically made a statement that was full of wisdom and from it we can gain much benefit. Imam Malik said:

"Anyone can be refuted in their argument and proven to be wrong except that man there!" He proceeded to point to the grave of the Messenger of Allaah (SAAWS)!

From this statement we clearly see that any "modern day scholar" is subject to error and thus, can be refuted if found to be incorrect. We also see, from this statement, the status that Prophet Muhammad (SAAWS) has with Allaah and the importance of his guidance for all of us, then and now.

Unfortunately and sadly, many of us want to elevate those leaders among us to this status where they can not be refuted. They won't even consider the possibility that perhaps these leaders may be wrong in their opinions and positions relative to the correct understanding and practice of matters in this deen, Islam.

ISLAM IN AMERICA 1995

Having said this, I will attempt to discuss the period in question in an accurate, brief and concise manner. In the bibliography at the end of this book, I have listed the publications and recordings used in researching this chapter as well as this book. I have also supplied a suggested reading list wherein one can find most of the authentic sources of Islamic information that were utilized in this project.

My intention is to simply analyze and critique the teachings of Wallace D. Muhammad during this period of time as it relates to what has happened since 1975. I will use the Quran and the authentic Sunnah as my sole criteria in refuting anything found in this analysis. In many instances, I will highlight, point by point, Wallace D. Muhammad's stated position at that time and then present the position of Allah and his Messenger (SAAWS).

None of the analysis or refutations are based on my opinion. This is not a personal attack. Islam is not based on anyone's logic, opinion or self interpretation. Everything in our religion has a text or a proof that can

20 YEARS A.E. (after Elijah)

determine it's validity or rejection as kufr (disbelief) or bidaa' (innovation).

As for the current leadership and teachings, we will use this same criteria in examining these issues in a later chapter. As you read this section, you should remind yourself to fear Allaah and ask for His guidance. If you disagree with anything that is rejected or refuted, then do as Allaah has commanded and BRING YOUR PROOF IF YOU ARE TRUTHFUL. Just make sure your "proof" is based on the best of proofs, the Quran and the authentic Sunnah of His Messenger (SAAWS).

Remember these words of Allaah in His Book, the Quran (translated):

"IN MATTERS WHEREIN YOU DIFFER, REFER IT BACK TO ALLAAH AND HIS MESSENGER!"

ISLAM IN AMERICA 1995

THE NATION LIVES ON.....

Before I begin to analyze the early teachings of Wallace D. Muhammad, I want to briefly discuss some of the highlights of his leadership during the first ten years. I find it necessary to take a look at some of the organizational changes that he made. Many of these changes have a direct relationship with his teachings and ideology of that time.

When he assumed leadership of the movement, the "Nation of Islam" was reported to have over 80 million dollars in holdings from real estate, farmland and other assets. But upon close examination, many of the movement's businesses and properties were debt ridden, and in some cases, they were in shambles and complete ruin. Much of this was due to the mismanagement, corruption and dishonesty on the part of various people that were entrusted with the affairs of the movement at various times.

To further complicate matters, Elijah Muhammad died without a will. The property of the movement became intertwined with his personal estate

20 YEARS A.E. (after Elijah)

and for over a decade, many of his twenty one (21) children (from his wife Clara and several other women) and the movement battled over these possessions. Wallace D. Muhammad had to make several major decisions. He began to systematically restructure and dismantle the "Nation of Islam" as it existed under Elijah Muhammad.

When he took over, in addition to unloading the burden of some of the unprofitable businesses, he also abolished some of the key rules and eliminated the policies that had been binding upon the members of the movement. One of the first things he did was stop making the weekly contributions that we mentioned earlier, obligations as they were referred to, mandatory. This was certainly a good thing, as this forced charity was nothing more than a distorted version of Zakat.

He also eliminated the sales quota for the newspaper. This quota used to be 300 copies a week, to be sold by each and every able-bodied male, the Fruit of Islam. In conjunction with this, he disbanded the Fruit of Islam and the woman's group, the Muslim Girls

Training and General Civilization Class. He also relaxed the dress code for the women. This was a major mistake, as in many cases, this was taken to the other extreme. As we will discuss in greater detail in a later chapter, this issue is still a major problem among his followers today.

Wallace D. Muhammad also closed many of the schools, known at that time as Muhammad's Universities of Islam. Many would reopen beginning in 1977 under the name Clara Muhammad Schools. He said that this was in honor of his mother, who was sincerely committed to education and concerned about the children. This name is still used today by the schools throughout the country which have been developed within the various communities that support his leadership.

The temples became known as mosques, and later, as masjids. Some semblance of Islam was beginning to emerge. In 1976, he renamed the movement "the World Community of Al-Islam in the West". He explained that this was an effort to align the old movement with the Muslims of the world. In 1980, he would again

20 YEARS A.E. (after Elijah)

rename the movement. The new name was the "American Muslim Mission", which he said more accurately reflected the goals and objectives of his leadership, and the ambitions of his followers.

In 1985, citing the problems with centralized leadership, he disbanded this group and said that he, Wallace D. Muhammad, was no longer the leader in a formal sense. He encouraged his followers to deal with their issues and concerns on a local and community level, and to support their respective leaders, who by this time were referred to as Imams. This is the correct name for the one who is responsible for leading the prayer, and in a general sense, responsible for the day to day religious affairs within the masjid.

During those first 5 years or so, there was a lot of change and movement within the organizations. As we will discuss later, some of these changes had an adverse effect not only on the followers of the new leadership, but on some of the personalities within the organization. This is very important to bear in mind as you proceed through this book. The changes that occurred during this period of time had an enormous impact upon the current state of Islam in America, and in many respects, many of us are still feeling the effects of those changes.

Wallace D. Muhammad was able to neutralize the existing power base within the movement that he inherited. This would enable him to basically operate unopposed. The common people among the membership, those who followed his father before him, considered him as one who was divinely sent!

Anything that he said or did, no matter if they understood it or not, they would have accepted it as the truth without a doubt and beyond reproach. He himself even proclaimed, as was printed on the front page of the movement's newspaper, that he was "born for the mission".

And the story is well known about how Fard, the false "prophet", allegedly "predicted" that Elijah Muhammad's wife Clara was pregnant with a boy, and Fard wrote the name of this unborn child on the door. The legend continues that Fard said that this child was a "special child", and he would one day help his father in his work.

I've said everything in these past few paragraphs simply to illustrate this next very important point. There was an unshakable level of devotion, support and blind following present under the leadership of Wallace D. Muhammad during that time. Again, Allaah had given him yet another opportunity to use this incredible influence and "power" to call the people to the correct understanding of Islam.

However, for years to follow after February 26, 1975 had come and gone, his teachings and leadership were filled with concepts, ideologies and understanding that were clearly and irrefutably contrary to the Quran and the understanding of Islam that is found in the authentic Sunnah of the Messenger of Allaah (SAAWS).

I will now proceed to present some of these concepts and teachings exactly as they were taught and explained by Wallace D. Muhammad during this period of time. Many of these lectures

ISLAM IN AMERICA 1995

I attended, and I will use the writings, lectures and other presentations that he made during this period. In addition to the documentation that I used which was publicly available and in some cases, can still be found, I will also for the first time in print, present and examine the concepts and teachings that were presented in Wallace D. Muhammad's "official Minister's kits".

These kits contain pages and pages of his teachings. They were only made available to the ministers that were directly responsible for temples, later called mosques, under his leadership. As I stated earlier, my father was one such minister. All praise is due to Allaah, he has moved completely away from this teaching and is a sincere believer, with a solid record of service to the Muslim community that continues to this day.

These Ministers kits used to arrive at our home, via certified mail, directly from the Chicago office of Wallace D. Muhammad on an almost quarterly schedule (i.e. January, April, June, etc.) for the first year and a half of his leadership. The first kit, which is in my possession, and I am referring to

20 YEARS A.E. (after Elijah)

it as I write these words, was dated April 1, 1975. The first page as you turned the cover reads exactly as follows:

"This Minister's kit has been made available to you by permission of the Honorable Wallace D. Muhammad, Supreme Minister of the Nation of Islam.

The information herein is for your study and mental digestion. IT IS NOT TO BE COPIED OR REPRODUCED IN ANY WAY."

So as you see, Allaah has allowed us to have more than enough information from which to present this subject. The question is, what new reasons or arguments will emerge from the people among us in defense of these things? Who will dare be arrogant enough to openly contend with Allaah and His Messenger (SAAWS) regarding what is guidance and what is error, what is kufr and what is iman, and what is sunnah and what is bidaa'?.

For the sake of clarity, I will divide the concepts and teachings of Wallace D. Muhammad during this period of time into categories. At the end of each category, I will give the correct Islamic viewpoint on these issues. Wherever possible, I will cite a verse of the Quran and/or an authentic hadith from Allaah's Messenger (SAAWS), that directly refutes the particular point or concept that is mentioned.

In the cases where this is not possible, this indicates that based on my research, there was no basis whatsoever in the Quran and Sunnah that could even be used to try to determine where this position came from. More clearly stated, the concept or position of Wallace D. Muhammad on some issues could not even be deemed a distorted or misguided understanding based on his interpretation of one of the authentic sources. The origin of his concepts are completely unknown in any "Islamic body of work", authentic or deviant!

THIS CLEARLY REFLECTS THAT THE VAST MAJORITY OF IDEAS, CONCEPTS, AND TEACHINGS EXPRESSED BY WALLACE D. MUHAMMAD DURING THIS PERIOD OF TIME WERE NEWLY INVENTED MATTERS INTO THE

20 YEARS A.E. (after Elijah)

DEEN OF ISLAM, AND CAN CLEARLY BE CLASSIFIED AS INNOVATIONS, BIDAA'. THIS IS NOT MY OPINION, THIS IS BASED ON THE FACTS PRESENTED AND JUDGED SOLELY BY THE QURAN AND THE AUTHENTIC SUNNAH OF THE MESSENGER OF ALLAAH (SAAWS).

Before the conclusion of this chapter, I will provide for the reader who may not be familiar with this issue, some of the most commonly heard arguments from the people who defend the use of these deviant and astray concepts. Some among us want to give certain individuals rights and exclusions that Allaah and His Messenger (SAAWS) have not given them!

I will present a response to all of these arguments, of course, based on the Quran and the Sunnah, and I will issue a challenge and propose a way to deal with this subject of the teachings of Wallace D. Muhammad during this period of time, once and for all, inshallah. And Allaah knows best. With that, I begin.

ISLAM IN AMERICA 1995

THE FIRST OFFICIAL INTERVIEW

The following information was taken from an interview conducted for Bilalian News newspaper, which was formally known as Muhammad Speaks, by Herbert Muhammad. He is now known as Jabir Muhammad, and is the brother of Wallace D. Muhammad. I am going to reprint, unedited, some of the key points of this interview.

This interview was identified as the "first official interview", and it was also reprinted in a book entitled *The Teaching of W.D. Muhammad, Book 'I, Secondary/Adult Level.* In this interview, and throughout the entire book, there are all kinds of concepts, interpretations and teachings, the likes of which I've never seen. Most of what is highlighted in this chapter can be found in this book.

B.N. (Bilalian News): Why were you chosen to succeed your father, rather than one of the elder brothers?

Chief Min. (Minister): "My personal answer would be it was God's intention. It was God's plan. But I

20 YEARS A.E. (after Elijah)

have also heard my father, himself, say that when I was born or I was conceived in my mother, he had been born as the Servant, the Messenger of God, Who manifested Himself with W.F. Muhammad; and my being born at the time when he was in contact with his Saviour, the God in Person, helped to inform me, not only as a child of his loins, but a child for the mission".

I seek refuge with Allaah from such speech!

Here, Wallace D. Muhammad is clearly committing shirk. He committed a major sin by saying that Allaah (he used the word God) manifested Himself in a human being. This is clearly and unquestionably against the essence of Islam.

B.N. You said you have been `groomed' by your father for this position. Why and for how long?

Chief Min.: "I have been groomed because it was necessary. Just being born of a body quickened by Divine Word was not enough. All the other spiritual leaders who had been chosen

ISLAM IN AMERICA 1995

for a great spiritual role and responsibility did not only have Divine Birth, but they also had the best qualified people to watch over their development-their religious development.

My father watched over my religious development and he had done that for as far back as I can remember."

In this response, he is making claims of divinity! He is also comparing his role to the roles of the prophets and messengers of Allaah. By him saying that he was chosen, as those before him, he had the best qualified people to watch over his development, he is giving credibility to Elijah Muhammad's teachings. This too, is contrary to Islam.

B.N.: As Chief Minister, will you have all of the powers that your father had, or does `not being the Messenger' imply that you will have less power and authority? If so, in what areas?

Chief Min.: "Well, I will ask those who would like to know more on this question to research or study the history of prophetic figures in the

20 YEARS A.E. (after Elijah)

Bible and Qur'an.

Moses was called the Prophet or Messenger of God, may peace be upon him, and Joshua came into that leadership. When Muhammad, the Holy Prophet of Arabia, physically passed away and spiritually returned to His God, the leadership remained. History shows it as a power equal or the same as that which existed under the personal supervision of that Arabian Prophet.

Messenger is a title. It speaks of or describes a birth and mission. That is, how that mission came to that man. One who inherits and is favored with the same support that is given to the Messenger has another name to describe him or to identify him is the stand as a title for him. That name or title for me is Chief Minister of the Nation of Islam. And my role is not that or a Messenger of God, but that of a "Mujeddid," meaning "One to watch over the new Islam" and to see that it is constantly and continually being renewed."

In this point, Wallace D. Muhammad again compared himself and his position to that of the prophets and messengers of Allaah! Notice how when he mentioned Moses, Musa, upon him be peace, he sent salutations but did not send any salutations whatsoever on the Messenger of Allaah (SAAWS) when he mentioned him! He also gives himself one of his many official titles, in fact, here he mentions two (2) of them; Chief Minister and Mujeddid. I personally know many people today, Muslims, who still use both of these titles when referring to him.

B.N.: Brother Minister, I noticed when you mentioned the Prophet Moses, you said: "May the peace of Allah be upon him." Will you teach your followers when they refer to the Honorable Elijah Muhammad to say this?

Chief Min.: Yes.

This statement speaks for itself! How can anyone on right guidance make such a statement. How can you take the salutations that are for Allaah's Messenger and apply them to a false prophet, a man who lied on Allaah and His Messenger (SAAWS) for over 40 years? Although the use of this salutation was eventually

20 YEARS A.E. (after Elijah)

changed to various other salutations that should only be used for Muslims (i.e., "may Allaah forgive him his sins and grant him Paradise"). again, I know of many others among us who still see nothing wrong with sending the salutation of the Messenger of Allaah (SAAWS) upon Elijah Muhammad. **This is ignorance and misguidance of the highest degree!**

B.N.: It is understood that the Hon. Elijah Muhammad, your father, stated that the Nation of Islam no longer turned towards the East for leadership. Will this be the prevailing policy or will the Nation seek leadership in the East?

Chief Min.: "It is true that the Hon. Elijah Muhammad taught us not to turn to the East for leadership. Turning to the East was symbolic. For the Sun rises in the East and the Sun brings us light to begin our day. This is symbolic of truth coming to the West from the East, but also prophesied that the Sun of Truth would rise in the West. The Hon. Elijah Muhammad's leadership and his work is the answer to that prophecy".

ISLAM IN AMERICA 1995

Here again, Wallace D. Muhammad is using some rational of his to say that our turning to the east, to the qiblaa', or the direction of prayer, was symbolic. More explicitly, he is saying that we should also not turn to the "east" for our guidance. Many people who follow him today use this statement when refusing to acknowledge the importance of the Sunnah. They use this statement and follow it up with professing to not follow any Arabs and to always follow leadership of one from among us! His statement of Elijah Muhammad being the fulfillment of prophecy does not even merit further discussion. As one can see by now, this type of misguidance was common place during that time.

B.N.: Would you explain to us how it is that you were once out of the Nation of Islam and all of your older brothers, who were never in discord with your father and his teachings have now accepted you totally as the leader of the Nation of Islam without any envy or jealousy of you. Would you say this is unusual?

Chief Min.: "No it is not unusual if you look at it from a scriptural

20 YEARS A.E. (after Elijah)

viewpoint. Joseph was sold into slavery and became a help to his community in Egypt. Moses was raised in the house of the Pharoah and acquired know-how that was needed by his people. It was Divinely planned that I should go out from the physical Nation of Islam to get those experiences necessary and come back to the Nation of Islam".

Once again, we see the claims of a divine plan, as if all of this is what Allaah has prescribed, as well as the comparisons with Allaah's prophets. Much of the same.

As clearly illustrated by the excerpts from that interview, the official position of Wallace D. Muhammad was based upon his own interpretation of the book of Allaah and his own ideological philosophies. The shirk and the other atrocities that he committed in this interview are an example of what his teachings reflected. As we will examine in these next sections, the fundamental foundation of his teachings were clearly in contradiction to the Quran and the authentic Sunnah of the Messenger of Allaah (SAAWS).

ISLAM IN AMERICA 1995

I will highlight the teachings of Wallace D. Muhammad exactly as they were presented. What makes matters worse, the majority of his teachings, concepts and ideologies that are presented in this chapter have also been compiled in a book entitled Wisdom from the West. This book, which was written by Muhammad Armiya Nu'Man, who is an Imam of one of the masjids from Imam W. Deen Mohammed's current community, is still being sold today. In fact, as we prepared to go to press, there is a picture on the front page of the Muslim Journal that shows another of the Imam's from this community proudly giving a relatively new Muslim a copy of this book, along with a cassette tape of a lecture given by Imam Mohammed!

If one does not still believe or support the misguided, deviant, innovated concepts and astray understanding presented in this book, why is it still being sold and promoted? If this community is in transition, why is it still calling the people to concepts and ideas that every single Muslim with even a basic, elementary level of Islamic education can clearly see are

20 YEARS A.E. (after Elijah)

against the guidance of the Quran and the Sunnah of the Prophet Muhammad (SAAWS)? There is no basis for any of these ideologies in the Quran or the Sunnah, so how can it be "wisdom", from the west, east or anywhere else?

In any event, this is the kind of situation that we were faced with during the first ten years of the leadership of Wallace D. Muhammad. It has evolved, as we will discuss in a later chapter, into a situation where even today, many people, including the Imams that represent the "ministry of Imam W. Deen Mohammed" (as it is known today), commonly refer to concepts and teachings from the first 10 years. They clearly know that these things are contrary to the Quran and the Sunnah. This is not the exception, this is the rule.

To continue, let's examine the teachings of Wallace D. Muhammad on various aspects of Islam, according to him.

ISLAM IN AMERICA 1995

CLAIMS OF DIVINITY

In April 1975, Wallace D. Muhammad outlined in clear detail many of his basic beliefs. At his first major public address entitled "Remake the World", witnessed by a crowd of over 25,000 people in Philadelphia. Pa., he made the following statements:

"The Muslims are now in the Body of Christ. You are the Second Christ. You are that Christ that has come in the end. Brothers and Sisters, go tell the church people that the Christ that they have been looking for to come down out of the clouds has already come down. Tell them in the words of their own Bible that it is not a flesh and blood body it's a city, a whole community.

Tell them they will not see any other Christ coming, this is the Christ. Tell them if they don't believe it, come to the head and find out... now Allah's light is coming to us and He has manifested His Presence in us...Brother and Sister don't look for Christ anymore, Christ is here".

I guess that what Allaah said in the Quran and what the Messenger of

20 YEARS A.E. (after Elijah)

Allaah said about Prophet Isa (Jesus peace be upon him), returning, praying behind him, dying and being buried by the Muslims doesn't matter to Wallace D. Muhammad. Not only did he interpret one of Allaah's prophets as an allegorical or symbolic concept, he committed shirk by saying that Allaah has manifested His presence in us! Astaghfirullah! I seek refuge with Allaah. This type of understanding negates the tawheed, nullifies the iman and can negate your Islam!

What would be his answer to the most basic question of "where is Allaah?" Based on his interpretation, like that of Elijah Muhammad (and today, Louis Farrakhan), it is acceptable to say that Allaah has "manifested" Himself in His creation! **This is clearly an astray understanding.**

Allaah has told us in numerous verses of the Quran and the Messenger of Allaah told us in numerous hadith that Allaah is above His throne, which is above the heavens! Nowhere does it ever say that Allaah is in the creation or that He exists within created beings.

ISLAM IN AMERICA 1995

DENIALS OF THE PROPHETS AND OTHER CLAIMS OF DIVINITY

This is excerpted from a speech given in Chicago four (4) years after the Philadelphia speech.

"Jesus did his work...He's not coming back here never! That's not the way of God. But his type has to return, another birth like his has to happen, has to happen, to produce his type again. So that his type will be able to see the lies that have been told concerning his birth. It's not him but it's the same as though he's the original. I know how Jesus is born because I've been born that way! So you can't tell me how Jesus was born, I've been born that way! What can you tell me about it? I know how Jesus came into the knowledge of revelation and how he got the knowledge of how to express and how to articulate-I've come through it myself. I know the signs, I have lived through them myself."

As we discussed in the last point, he continues to deny what Allaah and His Messenger (SAAWS) has said about the return of Isa (Jesus), peace

20 YEARS A.E. (after Elijah)

be upon him. In this statement, he also compared himself and his own human experiences with that of Jesus. He and the ignorant ones will rationalize that this is O.K., since Jesus is symbolic anyway! May Allaah guide those that are sincerely seeking the truth and right guidance.

INTERPRETATION OF THE BOOKS OF ALLAH WITH HIS OPINION

According to W.D. Muhammad in the talk given January 1978, he made the following statements regarding Adam, Eve and the interpretation of other aspects of the Qur'an and the Bible.

"Adam did not sin directly. It was the Nation (Eve) that was formed from him that sinned. After the members of society begin to listen to the serpent (Satan) and eat from corrupt guidance and knowledge, the leadership then feels that the only way to keep that leadership is to satisfy the society. So Eve (society) ate and she gave it to Adam. Adam ate to satisfy the society and to secure leadership for himself. In the absence of right guidance you will find weak leadership that will follow the masses or the public."

In another statement, he said: "the New Testament ruled the Christian world. The Torah ruled the Judaic world. The Holy Qur'an ruled the Islamic world. These scriptures were as Suns that ruled the world. In the Second Resurrection, we don't need the sun or the moon because God, Himself, will be the light. We will come to see Him face to face. We won't go to the Scripture for light. We go to God for light. Then we leave God and look at the Scripture and see more light. Scripture has not directed me. It is my sight upon the Image of Divine that has been the Light to dispel darkness from the pages of Scripture. God is already "the Light of the World" with me. It will take you time to come into the understanding of just how He is the Light of the World and why Scripture is not".

This statement is filled with things that we can address point by point, but the overall tone has already been established by his prior statements. What I will address here is this reference to a concept called the "Second Resurrection".

20 YEARS A.E. (after Elijah)

This term is used to define the end of the Nation of Islam and the beginning of the "transition" to Islam as defined by the Quran and the Sunnah. There are many people who refer to the time of "the Nation" as the "First Resurrection". **I want to make it perfectly clear for anyone who does not understand, that this reference to that time of ignorance as a "first resurrection" is a statement of kufr (disbelief)!**

Why? Because this is saying that what was taught by Elijah Muhammad is valid as the first stage of development for us to become Muslims! If we are now in the "second resurrection" which is supposed to reflect our "evolution", then the "first resurrection" would be valid Islamically as a foundation for the current process of "transition". This is false, astray and a definite reaffirmation of continued disbelief!

DENIAL OF THE MIRACLES OF THE QUR'AN

One of the major, common practices of Wallace D. Muhammad during this time and at various times was the denial of the miracles of the Quran. He has taken the position that the miracles were not real but rather allegorical, symbolic or metaphorical. This type of understanding is still present today, and is the reason why some of these so-called "knowledgeable Imams" who support his leadership, attack translations such as *The Noble Quran*.

This translation is the best English translation available. If anyone knows of a better one, then present it. *The Noble Quran* uses the authentic hadith to explain the meaning of the Quran as understood by the Messenger of Allaah (SAAWS).

Because these people would like to interpret and translate the Quran based on their understanding, and to make it suitable for their program, they ignorantly attack *The Noble Quran*. When these people write their articles and books and open their mouths to speak, Allaah makes it clear to all of us that these people have a poor understanding of Islam. Let's see what Wallace D. Muhammad has to say in his "interpretation" of the Quran, and then we can compare it to how the Messenger of Allaah

20 YEARS A.E. (after Elijah)

(SAAWS) understood it.

"Moses, being pursued by Pharaoh's army, struck the water and the Red Sea parted, so the Book says, and Moses and his people walked across on dry land...Brother and Sister you will never convert intelligent people to religion today with unrealistic symbolical stories like that. We do not see any sea parting now, no matter how holy the people are. If these are the kinds of "miracles" that God can performed, I am sure that as long as we have suffered and as much as we have cried in the name of Jesus...almighty God would have opened up some path for us or He would have produced some bridge for us to walk over out of America into a better land."

In another quote taken from a lecture in Detroit, Michigan in 1988, he gives his interpretation of the verse of the Quran where Allah speaks about making the fire cool and safe for Prophet Ibrahim. Observe what was said by Wallace D. Muhammad (by this time known as W. Deen Muhammad).

"We know that as much as man fears

the fire we know that Abraham was put in the fire. Yes Abraham was put in the fire. And when they looked in the fire when those who put him in the fire came to see how he was fairing, how he was doing there, whether he was ashes or not, they found him there unaffected. Fire hadn't touched him, fire hadn't bothered him a bit. Instead, instead of him experiencing heat, see God made the flame cool on Abraham (laughter). Now we know that's metaphorical, that's symbolic."

As Muslims, part of our belief is believing that whatever Allaah has said in His book, the Quran, is true. Any miracle or something that Allaah in His power made happen, regardless of whether our minds can comprehend it or not, we believe it happened! We don't question "How?", this is for Allaah to know. All He has to say is "Be" and it is. You can not claim to be a Muslim if you don't believe this basic fundamental point.

Now, regarding the previously mentioned point of Wallace D. Muhammad, Allaah has said in His Quran, His true, un-allegorical, un-metaphorical, un-symbolic book of

20 YEARS A.E. (after Elijah)

guidance, translated:

"(Abraham) said: "Do you then worship others besides Allaah, things that can neither profit you, nor harm you?"

"Fie upon you, and upon that which you worship besides Allaah! Have you then no sense?"

They said: "Burn him and help your gods, if you will be doing."

Allaah said: "O fire! Be you coolness and safety for Abraham!"

And they wanted to harm him, but We made them the worse losers.

Enough said!

DIFFERING WITH THE QUR'AN AND SUNNAH REGARDING OTHER ASPECTS OF AQEEDAH (BELIEFS)

"Muslims do not believe that there are some foreign worlds existing out there somewhere. We don't believe that there are some foreign creatures sharing space with us. We don't accept the notion of other creatures in another dimension whose nature is

ISLAM IN AMERICA 1995

not like ours. We don't believe that there are creatures who can do things to us but we cannot reach them unless we find some way to plug into their foreign dimension. The real Muslim cannot accept that idea. You cannot work voodoo on a Muslim because the Muslim is not vulnerable to superstition.

Allaah has said in the Quran (translated):

"NONE IN THE HEAVENS AND THE EARTH KNOWS THE UNSEEN BUT ALLAAH".

In another verse, Allaah has said (translated):

"I HAVE CREATED MEN NOR JINN BUT TO WORSHIP ME!"

The verses of the Quran and the authentic narration's of the Messenger of Allaah (SAAWS) are numerous and irrefutable as proof that we as Muslims are commanded to believe in the existence of the unseen. The angels, jinn's, and the unseen creation that is part of Allaah's creation are things that all Muslims have to believe in. It is not

20 YEARS A.E. (after Elijah)

even conceivable that someone can come to us and make us doubt what Allaah and His Messenger (SAAWS) have said regarding these issues.

Another issue where the position of Wallace D. Muhammad expresses an opinion that disobeys the commandments of Allaah and His Messenger (SAAWS) found both in the Quran and the Sunnah, is his negation of the Muslim woman's dress.

He gave a lengthy discourse filled with his "opinions" regarding this issue, but I will select the points in the discourse that clearly state his position.

He said "It is believed in the circle of learned scholars in the religion that the hair on women should be covered. It has been suggested that this is because men have associated sex appeal with practically every part of the woman. I accept that, I agree with that. But too, I accept that putting too much meaning or importance on the covering of hair has brought in a kind of suspicion or superstition surrounding women."

ISLAM IN AMERICA 1995

"In parts of Africa, women go with the breasts exposed, and there are additional places on the other side of the world where women may be seen with the breasts exposed. We usually associate it with primitive life. I don't think it's primitive at all. I think it's what people have become accustomed to and we can't say they are not moral because they go that way. If women in those cultures that are not religious, in the popular sense as we understand religion, to that way it is because they haven't attached any moral meaning to their breast yet".

He concluded by saying: "Here in our community, we don't make any big to-do about it. If some woman is seen with her hair uncovered we don't raise the roof, because I understand that where there is some sex appeal in women's hair, there is also religious symbolism attached. This symbolism is good, but I don't think that we should enforce these laws too fanatically. If we do, we might cause people of higher intellect to underestimate our intelligence. They might think we are superstitious or fanatical people and we don't want them to think that."

20 YEARS A.E. (after Elijah)

This statement sums up my entire presentation on the position and teachings of Wallace D. Muhammad as they relate to his contradicting the Quran and the authentic Sunnah. Allaah has said in the Quran (translated):

"AND TELL THE BELIEVING WOMEN TO LOWER THEIR GAZE, GUARD THEIR MODESTY, AND NOT TO SHOW OFF THEIR ADORNMENT EXCEPT WHAT IS APPARENT".

I don't think that anyone is of "higher intellect" than the sincere, believing Muslim, man or woman, who hears and obeys the commandments of Allaah and His Messenger. If Allaah has commanded his Messenger (SAAWS) to command the believing women to cover themselves, and we find the clear examples of this in the Sunnah, what gives anyone the right to lessen or negate this commandment by attaching symbolism to it?

What gives Wallace D. Muhammad more right than the Messenger of Allaah (SAAWS) to give his community a separate set of rules to live by that contradict the rules that the companions of the Messenger of Allaah (SAAWS), may Allaah be pleased with all of them, lived by? This is just a clear example of the danger of our own opinions when they are not based on the correct guidance.

So we find today, one can pick up any given issue of the *Muslim Journal* , and see Muslim women wearing all sorts of outlandish clothing, with no khimars (proper head covering) at all. Some are wearing hats, turbans or see through scarves ceremoniously draped over their heads (sliding hairpieces as I refer to them at times).

Their pictures appear in this paper and under the pictures, it is common to see such captions as "the cultural expression of a Muslim woman" or "the Muslim Women's Fashion Extravaganza", etc. Often times, these sisters form various groups and are portrayed in this paper as the representation of the Muslim American women. This couldn't be further from the truth.

Most of the Muslim women that I know of are some of the most sincere

20 YEARS A.E. (after Elijah)

Muslims that I know. They fear Allaah and it is evident that they are attempting to follow the commandments of Allaah and His Messenger (SAAWS) with respect to their conduct, dress and modesty. I can truthfully say that these are "beautiful" sisters and I've never seen any of their hair or other "symbolic"adornments!

I recall an incident last year where I was talking with a group of brothers. Among the group, 2 or 3 of the brothers were from the community of Imam W. Deen Mohammed and they consider him their leader. Somehow, we got on the subject of Muslim publications.

One of the brothers (and despite his lack of understanding, I still consider him my brother) said that we should support all of these publications. I agreed, but I said that we need to do our best to make sure that all of the images presented in these publications are Islamically correct, and in accordance with the Quran and the Sunnah.

The brother asked for an example. I cited the example that I've just

ISLAM IN AMERICA 1995

mentioned regarding the sisters not being dressed properly, as well as these "fashion shows" where the sisters are modeling and parading on stages in front of men, Muslims and non-Muslims alike. The brother vehemently and arrogantly disagreed with my position. When I cited the verses from the Quran that address this issue, do you know what his response was?!? He looked at the other brothers with an incredulous, surprised look, as if I had just arrived from outer space, and he said: **"Where have you been? Don't you know that the Imam changed all of that!"**

When I began to clearly and intelligently explain to him how this position was not Islamically correct, he boldly proclaimed that **"if it wasn't for Imam W. Deen Mohammed, we wouldn't even be Muslims.** Guys like you would be scared to come out and say that you're a Muslim if it wasn't for 'the Imam'." Look at the level of ignorance that blind following creates. It can even lead a person to make statements of kufr, without even realizing it! This kind of statement is

20 YEARS A.E. (after Elijah)

not an uncommon thing.

At that point, the brothers who were with me admonished me to end the conversation, because they could see that in my defense of Islam, of Allaah and His Messenger (SAAWS), I was becoming increasingly stronger in my position, whereas the brother was clearly rejecting my argument, in spite of the proofs that he was presented with.

Before concluding this chapter with a few statements from the Minister's kits of Wallace D. Muhammad that we mentioned earlier, I'd like it to be perfectly clear that my position now is the same as my position on that day last summer! Anyone or anything that is in clear conflict with what Allaah and His Messenger (SAAWS) have brought, they should be and will be rejected, then and now! I wouldn't care if he calls himself the supreme minister, the royal Imam, the grand poobah, or the Muslim pope.

Allaah has said in the Quran (translated):

"BUT NO! BY YOUR LORD! THEY CAN HAVE NO FAITH UNTIL THEY

MAKE YOU A JUDGE IN ALL DISPUTES BETWEEN THEM, AND FIND IN THEMSELVES NO RESISTANCE AGAINST YOUR DECISIONS, AND ACCEPT THEM WITH FULL SUBMISSION".

Again, the laws of Islam are everlasting and undiscriminating. They apply to EVERYONE! Then and now. As I said when beginning this chapter, this was the most difficult part of the book for me to write. I had access to so much information and there is so much more that I could have written. The Minister's kits that were prepared by Wallace D. Muhammad are filled with all sorts of astray and misguided concepts. Most of these things I wouldn't want to subject the readers with having to read.

But as an example of what is contained in these kits, before ending this chapter with a challenge to Wallace D. Muhammad, the man who is known today as Imam W. Deen Mohammed, I will provide an excerpt from the Minister's kit of April 1, 1975. This statement, though it was written over 20 years ago has never been formally retracted, as most of

20 YEARS A.E. (after Elijah)

the teachings during this time have never been publicly denounced by him.

This statement set the tone for the teachings that we have just discussed which occurred during the first 10 years of his leadership and beyond. It proves that certainly what is built upon falsehood is itself falsehood.

He began this kit by saying: "In the name of Allah, the Beneficent, the Most Merciful, To Whom we forever give Praise and Thanks for His blessing us with a Black Saviour. One who met and became a Saviour because God in the Person manifested Himself. He met that One in the person of the Great Master W. F. Muhammad. We forever thank Him for the great blessing of the Honorable Master Elijah Muhammad."

He made the following claim on page 77 of this same kit in a section entitled "The "D" in W. D. Muhammad: "The "D" stands for prayer. That prayer we call "Abraham's prayer." "Oh Allah, exalt Muhammad and the followers of Muhammad". The "D" is given to

ISLAM IN AMERICA 1995

"Me" because that's the job of the One in this day and time: "To bring to fullness or to (the) realization (of) the prayer of Abraham. The Great Master W. F. Muhammad brought that "D" because that is the job. The one who bears that "D" is the answer to that prayer. He's the One who works for that prayer to see that it is a reality."

I could go on further, but I think that I've said more than enough to clearly illustrate this issue. Now, among the arguments that we will hear, as we've heard for so long now, is why have I highlighted these things? "The Imam" has grown since then". Alhamdulillah if he has grown. The problem is, among his followers, including the Imams that support his leadership, many still stand by these teachings and espouse these ideas and concepts. This is evidenced by, as I pointed out earlier, that as recently as now, May 1995, books are still being sold that highlight and support these teachings and concepts in detail!

Imam W. Deen Mohammed either openly condones these teachings by allowing these books to continue to be sold and promoted among his

125

20 YEARS A.E. (after Elijah)

"followers", or he is implying his approval of this by remaining silent, as silence is tacit approval. I also know of some Imams that still, twenty years after the emergence of this leadership and these teachings, in the face of the wealth of Islamically sound information that we've been blessed with, base their taaleems and introduction to Islam classes on the early books of Wallace D. Muhammad Books such as *the Teachings of W. D. Muhammad, the Lectures of Emam Muhammad, An African-American Genesis* and many of his other books and presentations are clearly deviant and not in accordance with the Quran and the authentic Sunnah at all, and this is a fact that no one can dispute!

So I am aware of all the arguments. There was a time, before Allaah (and no one else) allowed me to really begin to understand Islam that I could present these arguments or positions in support of Wallace D. Muhammad probably as well as, or better than any of these Imams and other individuals who currently support him!

Allaah delivered me from darkness

ISLAM IN AMERICA 1995

and showed me enough light to allow me to become more firm in His deen. So, I was able to move away from ALL of the things that I had learned under Elijah Muhammad up until 1975, and under Wallace D. Muhammad during the period of time that we have just discussed in this chapter.

After knowledge has come, we as Muslims are obligated and commanded by Allaah and His Messenger (SAAWS) to repent, change our belief, conduct, speech and actions. Then we must begin practicing this religion of Islam as given to us by Allaah in the Quran and as understood and practiced by the Messenger of Allaah, Prophet Muhammad (SAAWS), his companions, and all those who follow that guidance until the Last Day.

This is my challenge to Imam W. Deen Mohammed and all of those that follow his leadership:

If Imam W. Deen Mohammed has repented to Allaah, as we are commanded to do, for all of the things that he said which are against Allaah, any of His messengers or prophets, or

20 YEARS A.E. (after Elijah)

anything else that he has said that is clearly against the correct understanding of Islam, then alhamdulillah, and this is between him and Allaah.

However, it is also his obligation to publicly denounce these teachings in a clear and concise manner. Not vaguely, but specifically. This is binding upon ANY leader who has said something, or called the people or their followers to anything that was not Islamically correct.

Imam Mohammed should IMMEDIATELY order the removal of any books, tapes or other publications that contain any statements that are contrary in belief or practice, to the Quran and the authentic Sunnah. This is especially important, as many innocent people are still being affected by things that he said 20 years ago! Why? Because he allows the people that claim to follow him to continue promoting these things, even in his own communities' newspaper.

He should begin to make it a requirement for any Imam that supports his leadership to use the Quran and the authentic Sunnah in their efforts of carrying out their responsibilities within the communities across the country. They should stop interpreting the Quran with no proofs for their claims and no correct understanding of the Quran, and they should immediately stop using weak, unauthentic and forged hadith, lying on the Messenger of Allaah (SAAWS)!

If these basic, simple steps are taken, then we as Muslims are obligated not to bring up any of the teachings or statements that he has made in the past. If Imam W. Deen Mohammed fulfills these basic, but important responsibilities to Allaah and Islam, he would have to be accepted at his word.

But as long as the things that were taught from 1975 through 1985, and in some cases beyond that time are still allowed, then he, Imam W. Deen Mohammed is still is conflict with the Quran and the authentic Sunnah. This is not MY opinion, this is based on the best of guidance, the book of Allaah, the Quran and the authentic Sunnah of Prophet Muhammad (SAAWS). If he discharges this responsibility, it would not be

20 YEARS A.E. (after Elijah)

acceptable for anyone to bring up the past. Until this is done, it is only proper for us to think that he still stands by those things. I sincerely pray Allaah that this is not the case.

As for those whom I know personally that support his leadership, I still love you for the pleasure of Allaah, and I pray Allaah that he makes the road to the truth and the straight path easy for you. I pray that Allaah grants you the ability to see the difference between and distinguish truth from falsehood, guidance from error, and give you to courage to judge everything, everyone and what they are leading to, by the Quran and the Sunnah, before the Quran and the Sunnah judges you!

As one of the illustrious companions of our Prophet Muhammad (SAAWS), Umar ibn Al-Khattab said:

"TAKE ACCOUNT OF YOURSELVES BEFORE YOU ARE TAKEN ACCOUNT OF. WEIGH YOUR SCALES BEFORE THEY ARE WEIGHED FOR YOU, AND PREPARE YOURSELF FOR THE GREAT GATHERING".

ISLAM IN AMERICA 1995

I ask this from Allah for myself, and for all the Muslims who are sincerely seeking this truth. I ask this of Him, I repent to Him and I ask Him to forgive us all. Ameen.

20 YEARS A.E. (after Elijah)

CHAPTER FIVE   BREAKING AWAY...LOUIS FARRAKHAN GOES SOLO

One of the most visible personalities to emerge from the movement under Elijah Muhammad's leadership was Louis Farrakhan. Today, he is known among his followers and to the world as "the Honorable Minister Louis Farrakhan".

Born Louis Eugene Walcott, Farrakhan joined Elijah Muhammad's movement in 1955. Much has been written concerning his background, his relationship with Malik Shabazz, etc. Much can be said to gain more of an understanding of a man like Louis Farrakhan, but space does not allow for a detailed history. But I do feel it is important that you have some background of Farrakhan as it relates to our subject.

When Wallace D. Muhammad assumed the leadership of "the Nation" Farrakhan was one of his strongest supporters. He also served as the spokesperson under this new leadership. He was moved from New York where he had been since succeeding Malik Shabazz (then still known as Malcolm X) as the Minister of Temple #7. He came to Chicago to establish a new mosque on the west side under the direction of the new leadership. In 1976, Farrakhan was given a new name by Wallace D. Muhammad. He accepted the name "Abdul Haleem Farrakhan".

Many probably do not remember, but I've talked with some of the brothers who are from New York who were around then and they recall my account of Farrakhan clearly. Even before he left New York to go to Chicago, he was clearly not the same Farrakhan that represented Elijah's program in "the Nation".

He seemed more reserved, even restrained at times. He was definitely less visible than he had been. He was receiving less press in the media and his public speaking appearances were few. Whereas during "the good ol' days" everytime you looked up he was speaking somewhere, weekly, sometimes more than once a week. Now, you hardly heard of him speaking anywhere.

His physical appearance was even different. He wore a short Afro

20 YEARS A.E. (after Elijah)

hairstyle and even grew a beard, not a full, flowing beard, but clearly a beard nonetheless.

I remember in 1976, he was the guest speaker at a fund raising dinner that the mosque in Elizabeth had sponsored. As I mentioned earlier, my father enjoyed a good relationship with Farrakhan. In addition to being the National Representative, he also was responsible for the Eastern region. He helped facilitate my father's communication with the national leadership, was instrumental in helping my father solidify things structurally and gain recognition for his work as a Minister and then as an Imam under Wallace D. Muhammad.

He attended this dinner, I spoke with him, he interacted with the people there and was very friendly. I remember feeling that he would be an important asset in helping the new leadership in its' goals and objectives. Later, I would learn Farrakhan was having some difficulties with "the transition" even at that time. As we mentioned in the previous chapter, Wallace D. Muhammad was making many changes.

ISLAM IN AMERICA 1995

What particularly bothered Farrakhan was how Wallace was handling his father's image. Specifically, Elijah was no longer being viewed with the same esteem that he had been. Whereas he had always been referred to as "the Messenger", "Dear Holy Apostle" or some other lofty title, he was now being depicted in the role of "social reformer".

This of course, would also affect the status that Farrakhan held with the people. The new leadership began to focus less on personalities, and with Farrakhan being accustomed to almost celebrity status, he clearly felt out of place.

Farrakhan still believed that the program of Mr. Muhammad was the best program and that the movement should stay the course. He was also used to a certain lifestyle under the former leadership. He always traveled with an entourage; he went everywhere first class and enjoyed the best of the dunya (worldly things).

 He spent thousands of dollars on such frivolous things as violins. Under the new leadership all of these

20 YEARS A.E. (after Elijah)

things would cease to exist. In essence, he was taken from the most visible and influential area in the country, New York, and was placed on the west side of Chicago to toil in obscurity!

In 1976 after he transferred Farrakhan out of Temple #7 in New York, Wallace D. Muhammad renamed the temple Malcolm Shabazz, in honor of El Hajj Malik Shabazz. Remember, Farrakhan was this man's sworn enemy during his break with Elijah Muhammad. If there was ever a doubt as to the changes that Wallace D. Muhammad had in mind, this had to certainly show Farrakhan that there was a new boss in town.

During the time before Farrakhan left New York in June of 1975, my father went to visit him at his office at Temple #7. He visited at least once, sometimes two or three times a week. They sat and talked with each other extensively and discussed the movement and the plans of the new leadership, its' direction, etc.

One thing that stands out among all of the misguided teachings of "the

ISLAM IN AMERICA 1995

Nation of Islam" during Elijah Muhammad's time is the concept of the white man being the devil. And probably no one could espouse or preach this doctrine during that time better than Louis Farrakhan. So this next point is very important.

One day while my father was in Farrakhan's office he had confided in my father that he did not understand a lot of the things that Wallace was doing. While they were talking, a special news report came over the radio. The reporter said that Wallace D. Muhammad, the leader of the Nation of Islam has reversed the movement's policy of membership of blacks only. He has announced that all are welcome for membership, including whites.

Remember, during Mr. Muhammad's time, this was unthinkable. The fundamental appeal of the movement was that the black man was superior and that the white man was inferior. Now, Farrakhan was learning for the first time that the people he had preached were nothing but untrustworthy, deceitful, savage, blue-eyed devils, would now be his equal. He looked at my father and my

20 YEARS A.E. (after Elijah)

father recalled that he became pale, almost faint. His only reaction was "you have to please excuse me brother, but I have to go and lie down".

Shortly thereafter, he was transferred to Chicago. In his place, Jeremiah Shaheed Muslim Shabazz, (formerly known as Jeremiah X) would come from the Philadelphia temple. This temple had a history of corruption and a strong criminal element was present there (as evidenced by the tragedy with the Washington D.C. murders that we discussed earlier).

When Jeremiah came to New York and became responsible for the Eastern region, my father had to interact with him regularly. He recalls that when Jeremiah would call Chicago to speak with Wallace D. Muhammad on certain issues, sometimes Farrakhan would answer the telephone. He was a special aide to Wallace D. Muhammad when he went to Chicago.

Jeremiah would ridicule Farrakhan in front of my father and other people in the office. He would say things like "Look at him now. The great Louie

Khan, nothing but an office boy for Wallace Muhammad".

I have said all this to show how different things were for Abdul Haleem Farrakhan under the leadership of Wallace D. Muhammad. Oh how life was much sweeter for him when he was Louis Farrakhan! What is also important to note is that while in Chicago, Farrakhan also shared the responsibility of teaching the Minister's class. He along with Dr. Na'im Akbar would teach classes supposedly based on the understanding of the Quran and the teachings of Wallace D. Muhammad.

Farrakhan has always had some understanding of the Arabic language, having studied for many years under people like the late Arabic instructor and one time secretary for El Hajj Malik Shabazz when he was still Malcolm x, Maceo Hazziez. This is what makes him the worst of deviants and especially dangerous as we will discuss in the following chapter.

So, for a period of two years, Abdul Haleem Farrakhan worked along with Wallace D. Muhammad as Muhammad began his plan of action

20 YEARS A.E. (after Elijah)

for the movement. Finally, after two years of being in the background and struggling with the direction of the movement, in 1977, he went to Wallace D. Muhammad and told him he had tried to go along with him, but he could no longer do so. They then parted ways, amicably by all accounts.

Farrakhan would lay low for about a year. He said that he didn't leave with any plans on starting an organization. He even considered going back into the entertainment business (maybe going back to where it all began as `Calypso Gene, the Charmer') in an effort to support himself and his family. But in September 1977 in Los Angeles, he met with a man named Bernard Cushmeer, a writer and also a member of the movement during Elijah Muhammad's time. Farrakhan said that Cushmeer gave him a book that he had written. When he read that book, Farrakhan said: "I was so inspired that I decided, at that moment, to rebuild the work of the Honorable Elijah Muhammad."

He went "underground" for a period of time, met with his advisors and they called every minister that served

ISLAM IN AMERICA 1995

under Elijah Muhammad in an attempt to gain support. When they contacted my father and told him of Farrakhans' plans, he said that he was going to remain with Wallace D. Muhammad. A number of people 'defected' and either joined Farrakhan, set up movements of their own (i.e. Silis Muhammad and his version of the "Nation of Islam", based in Atlanta) or faded into oblivion (i.e., Jam Muhammad, Elijah Muhammad's look-alike brother).

Abdul Haleem Farrakhan would get a haircut, shave his beard, put on his silk suit and bow tie again and change his name back to Louis Farrakhan. As we will examine in full detail in the following chapter, the business of shirk and misguidance is alive and well; the Khan is back!

20 YEARS A.E. (after Elijah)

CHAPTER SIX: MINISTER LOUIS FARRAKHAN AND THE 'NEW AND REVIVED' NATION OF ISLAM

"I WILL PROVE TO YOU WITH THE HELP OF GOD THAT IT IS A PLEASURE TO FACE THE CROSS FOR THE GLORIFICATION OF MASTER FARD MUHAMMAD AND HIS CHRIST, THE MOST HONORABLE ELIJAH MUHAMMAD FOR YOUR REDEMPTION".

The above statement is from none other than Louis Farrakhan. It is excepted from a speech that he gave this year, on February 25, 1995 at a graduation and awards ceremony in Chicago.

This speech came one day before he gave his "Saviour's Day" address which was entitled "Jesus Saves!".

This is just one glaring example of the corrupted teachings of Louis Farrakhan and his "Nation of Islam". When he separated from Wallace D. Muhammad in 1978, he quietly began his "mission" which he said was to "restore the work of the Honorable Elijah Muhammad and lead the rise of the Nation." In the process, he has taken the deviance, shirk and misguidance of Elijah Muhammad to a new level!

What makes him even worse in my opinion, is that he has for years claimed to be Muslim, professed belief in Allah and in the Prophet Muhammad (SAAWS). Since his return, he has on numerous occasions traveled throughout various Muslim countries and has had audiences with many so-called Muslim leaders. In this chapter, I will spare no detail in exposing what Farrakhan really is.

It is very important to me that Louis Farrakhan and his impact on what has happened to the Muslims since 1975 be fully examined. This is due to a number of reasons. **One of the most disturbing comments made by Imam W. Deen Mohammed (formally known as Wallace D. Muhammad) was his 1993 endorsement of Farrakhan as a valid Muslim leader!** This appeared in an article in the New York Times in May of 1993, less than 2 years ago. This article was one of a series of articles that examined the Muslims of America.

20 YEARS A.E. (after Elijah)

Imam Mohammed's statement, as printed was as follows:

"AS FAR AS I'M CONCERNED, THERE ARE 2 MUSLIM LEADERS IN AMERICA. LOUIS FARRAKHAN IS THE LEADER FOR THE PEOPLE OF THE OLD WAYS AND I AM THE LEADER FOR THE CHANGE".

This is a very sad development and it should be disturbing to any and all of the Muslims of America, especially those that are striving our best to practice Islam correctly and to follow the Sunnah of Allaah's Messenger (SAAWS). Imam Mohammed's position is a very dangerous position and it makes our job of giving the correct dawah even more difficult. Why do I say this? It is because the ignorant, misinformed person can be led to believe that there is nothing wrong with what Louis Farrakhan preaches.

All of us, (or I should say most of us) as Muslims, we know better. We have clear guidelines by which to measure whether or not a person is a Muslim leader. There are thousands of examples in the Quran and in the authentic Sunnah for us to use. Based

ISLAM IN AMERICA 1995

on what Allaah gives us in the Quran and what Prophet Muhammad (SAAWS) left us from his Sunnah, one can clearly, without a doubt see that this man, Louis Farrakhan, is no more a Muslim leader than Jesse Jackson, Al Sharpton or any of these other nationalist, disbelieving "leaders" in America.

How can one even mention the words Louis Farrakhan, Muslim and leader in the same sentence?! Coming from a person like Imam W. Deen Mohammed, this is a very dangerous and misleading statement. Because of the influence that Imam Muhammad has on public opinion in this country, his "endorsement" of a person or a position holds a lot of importance. He is still considered by many, especially those in the popular media, as the leader of the Muslims in America.

Because of this endorsement of Farrakhan and other questionable and incorrect positions that he has taken relative to Islam even recently, in a later chapter I will have to provide a close examination of Imam W. Deen Mohammed and his "ministry". But for now, continuing,

20 YEARS A.E. (after Elijah)

let us look at what Farrakhan has been up to since going solo and taking his show back on the road.

He began speaking again in various cities throughout the country. People were beginning to get excited about his return. One of the biggest questions asked among the general public during this time was: "What has happened to the Muslims?" As we mentioned earlier, the "Nation of Islam" was the popular public perception of the Muslim and Islam. So Farrakhan sought to tell the world that the boys were back in town.

His first major event was his first visit to New York City since he was transferred to Chicago ten years earlier. The venue was the world famous Madison Square Garden. On October 7, 1985, 25,000 turned out to hear him speak. The atmosphere was almost like old times again for Farrakhan, except that this time it was his show and his show only. "Malcolm" was gone, Elijah was gone, he was away from Wallace; he was off and running.

His doctrine was the same as it ever was, circa 1965. The black

ISLAM IN AMERICA 1995

man is superior; we don't believe in a mystery God; the white man is the devil; all of the standard lies and falsehoods were still intact. The noticeable difference was that now, he began to speak of himself in prophetic or divine terms. He began to talk about how he should be compared to Jesus (Prophet Isa, on him be peace). He said that as the Jews were after Jesus that they were also after him today, and that he was on a divine mission. He rambled on and on for over three hours!

This showing in New York would be just what he needed to catapult him back into the national spotlight. He began to systematically restore every single aspect of Elijah Muhammad's program. He started a newspaper called *The Final Call*. He began to open up temples, which he calls mosques, in all of the cities that had temples in the original "Nation of Islam". They even used the identical numbers. Newark was Mosque #25, New York was #7, etc. He set up the same national structure, with a few modifications, and of course, he sat in the big seat.

He started actively trying to

20 YEARS A.E. (after Elijah)

reacquire all of the properties that had been sold or lost when Wallace D. Muhammad assumed the leadership. He even reacquired the home that Elijah Muhammad moved into in 1973, known as "the Palace". He paid 500,000 for it after paying off the delinquent taxes. He even paid $2.3 million dollars to acquire the temple that was the cornerstone of the movement, a former Greek orthodox church in Chicago. With the major props in place, **Farrakhan has firmly established himself as the leader of the "Nation of Islam". And his brand of shirk is new and improved and more astray than ever!**

Allaah has given us the following verses in the Quran as a perfect example of people such as Louis Farrakhan. Allaah states (translated):

"WHEN ASKED TO BELIEVE AS OTHERS DO, THEY SAY: 'SHOULD WE BELIEVE LIKE FOOLS?' AND YET THEY ARE THE FOOLS, EVEN THOUGH THEY DO NOT KNOW. WHEN THEY MEET THE FAITHFUL THEY SAY: `WE BELIEVE;' BUT WHEN ALONE

ISLAM IN AMERICA 1995

WITH THE DEVILS (THEIR COMPANIONS) THEY SAY: `WE ARE REALLY WITH YOU; WE WERE ONLY JOKING'.

BUT ALLAAH WILL TURN THE JOKE AGAINST THEM AND ALLOW THEM TO SINK DEEPER INTO EVIL AND WANDER IN THEIR WICKEDNESS. THEY ARE INDEED THOSE WHO BARTERED AWAY GOOD GUIDANCE FOR ERROR AND GAINED NOTHING FROM THE DEAL, NOR FOUND THE RIGHT WAY."

Surely the book of Allaah is the best speech and only those who seek to go astray and lead others astray will deviate from the light of the Quran and the best guidance given to us by Allaah in the authentic Sunnah of His Messenger, Prophet Muhammad (SAAWS).

20 YEARS A.E. (after Elijah)

FARRAKHAN INTO THE 90's.....THE BEAT GOES ON

As we entered into the 1990's, the program of Farrakhan was more of the same brand of kufr (disbelief). His movement began to go even further astray. He was still celebrating "Saviour's Day" not once a year, but twice a year! He celebrates on October 7th of each year to commemorate the birthday of Elijah Muhammad, whom he also refers to as a saviour. This is in addition to still perpetuating the lie of Fard Muhammad on February 26th of each year.

His celebrations are not just limited to Chicago. In 1994, he convened the October convention in Ghana! His shirk knows no geographic boundaries. These celebrations, as well as other gatherings that his movement sponsors, are filled today with more pageantry and spectacle than ever before. They never have an event without some entertainer or singer, sometimes 2 or 3 singers, putting on some elaborate stage show. Often times, there is someone singing a song in tribute to Farrakhan. Once

ISLAM IN AMERICA 1995

again, the business of shirk and misguidance is alive and well, and now it's even accompanied by dinner and a show. A full entertainment value!

As in the past, within Farrakhan's "Nation" today, there is still no correct practice or implementation of any of the duties required of the Muslim. All of the basic fundamentals of Islam are missing and/or completely corrupted by Farrakhan. There is no salat, zakat, and the fasting is corrupt. They are so astray they have corrupted the concept of Ramadan, the month of fasting that comes once a year in Islam.

In December, they fast and call it "Ramadan" as the followers of Elijah Muhammad did before them. They also "fast" during the correct time of Ramadan so as to align themselves falsely with the Muslims. I deliberately placed Ramadan and fasting in quotes when I referred to Farrakhan's practice, as fasting is for Allaah, and if one's concept and understanding of Allaah is astray and deviant, can this be considered fasting?

20 YEARS A.E. (after Elijah)

One of the most important things to note about Farrakhan is his ability to always say "the right words for the right audience". This is one of the reasons why I stated earlier that any respected Muslim endorsing or supporting Farrakhan, either openly or implicitly, is a dangerous thing. This is clearly an affront to the deen of Islam, the religion with Allaah.

Let us cite some examples of how the verses from the Quran that were noted in the last section apply to Farrakhan. On February 24, 1991, not long ago, he gave a speech at Christ Universal Temple on the topic: "Who is God?" Observe some of his remarks:

"HE IS NOT A SPIRIT, HE'S NOT A SPOOK. GOD IS REAL, HE IS A REAL LIVE HUMAN BEING, DIFFERENT FROM YOU AND ME ONLY IN THAT HE IS SUPREME IN KNOWLEDGE, WISDOM, UNDERSTANDING AND POWER."

He went on to further plunge into this ignorance and he restated his belief regarding the basis of "the Nations" doctrine of disbelief, then and now! He expounded on point #12, which was printed on the back of each and every copy of Muhammad Speaks newspaper. This statement is still being printed on the inside back cover of each and every edition of the Final Call. (It used to be printed on the back cover, but after Farrakhan made "Hajj" in the late 1980's and lied to the Muslims in Mecca that he had removed this point off of the paper, he conveniently moved it to the inside back cover!).

Point #12 reads as follows (and we seek refuge with Allaah):

"WE BELIEVE THAT ALLAH (GOD) APPEARED IN THE PERSON OF MASTER W. FARD MUHAMMAD, JULY 1930; THE LONG-AWAITED "MESSIAH" OF THE CHRISTIANS AND THE "MAHDI" OF THE MUSLIMS."

Please carefully read Farrakhan's words (which are reprinted and unedited as they appeared in the Final Call dated March 11, 1991):

"I shall never take that point from the back page of our paper, regardless to how many scholars don't like it. I visited Mecca and I sat with the

20 YEARS A.E. (after Elijah)

scholars and this was the main point that we wrangled over. But when we finished, the scholars recognized that they had never heard exposition like that. So, I figured that what I gave to them I should give to you. Since in Mecca they could not defeat me in my argument, and every argument they gave me I gave back to them with more detail, yet I am born in America, and never have been taught in any Islamic school by any scholars or scientists. I was taught by the Unlearned One, the Honorable Elijah Muhammad, but he doesn't make any fools!"

This vile, repugnant and ignorant discourse alone should be enough for anyone to conclude that Farrakhan is far, far astray and outside of the fold of Islam! His statements in this speech, as well as the things that he is saying today, as of this writing, are against the very fundamental core of Islam.

It certainly doesn't take any serious level of Islamic knowledge or scholarship to determine that this doctrine is pure, unadulterated shirk! No one can ever make me accept Louis Farrakhan as a Muslim, let

ISLAM IN AMERICA 1995

alone as a Muslim leader.

All of this came less than 6 months after he addressed an audience of over 700 Imams and other leaders of Muslim organizations from all over the country at the 2nd General Assembly of the Continental Council of Masajid. At this conference, he sat on the same podium with Imam W. Deen Mohammed, Imam Siraj Wahhaj from Brooklyn, NY and others.

In his speech, Farrakhan began by making the shahada, (the declaration of faith that one makes to enter into Islam) and he went into his usual rhetoric about how he wanted to work with the Imams and how his followers are "evolving". Again, he went into his bag of tricks and disguises and pulled out one of his "Muslim" speeches, as this was the audience for today's performance.

The people in attendance seemed to accept him and take him on his word. Now we see the results of that "trust". In no time at all, Farrakhan is right back to business as usual. In my few short years on Allaah's earth, I've never seen or heard someone lie on

20 YEARS A.E. (after Elijah)

Allaah, His book the Quran, His Prophet Muhammad (SAAWS) and on Islam so blatantly and boldly as this man! The position that the majority of the Muslims take as this deviant runs all over the country and the world committing these crimes and propagating this falsehood is to ignore him. All the while, he is steadily leading innocent, unsuspecting people astray.

We know as Muslims that whomever Allaah guides, no one can misguide, and whomever has been misguided, only Allaah can guide. This still does not absolve us of our obligation and responsibility to fight against ignorance and deviance concerning Islam. If we can't change this evil with our hands then we should speak against it. If we can't speak against it, we should hate it in our hearts. And as the hadith of Allaah's Messenger (SAAWS) tells us, this is the weakest of faith.

Some of us even go a step further. Not only do we not hate it in our hearts, we endorse him and classify him as a Muslim leader! I seek refuge with

ISLAM IN AMERICA 1995

Allaah from cowardliness and ignorance.

The Messenger of Allaah (SAAWS) told us in an authentic hadith:

"A BELIEVER IS NOT STUNG TWICE BY SOMETHING OUT OF ONE AND THE SAME HOLE!"

How many times are we going to be duped and misled into accepting people as Muslims and as leaders when their deeds, actions or their words don't reflect the proper understanding of Islam as defined by the Quran or the Sunnah? Is the only criteria for leadership that one has a large following or a large group of people following along blindly?

As Muslims, we should be aware and secure in the fact that the majority of the people have never been on the haqq (the truth). It has always been a small group of people holding on tenaciously to this truth. Power and strength in Islam is not based on numbers. So don't be fooled for one moment and believe that just because someone uses a few "Islamic" phrases and commands a following that that person can be deemed "a Muslim

20 YEARS A.E. (after Elijah)

leader."

There is so much more that can be said in an effort to expose the lie that is Louis Farrakhan. Inshallah, much more will be said in the future, and we will fulfill our responsibility in this dawah and educate the people who really do not know what isn't Islam. As for those who do know but just won't submit (as many of the Muslims are guilty of), at a certain point, you have to let them dwell in their own ignorance! But for sure, if an influential and widely respected Muslim endorses, as a Muslim leader, a man whose speech, actions and entire program is in opposition to Islam, one has to question the level of understanding of a Muslim who gives that endorsement.

I personally ask Allaah that He allow me to use my limited knowledge of the Quran and the Sunnah and call the people to the "real" Islam, which is the only Islam. There is no two "Islams", or two groups, the "old ways" and "the change"! Where is the evidence in the Quran and Sunnah of such a thing? There is Islam, as defined by Allaah and His Messenger (SAAWS) and there is falsehood.

ISLAM IN AMERICA 1995

Until I return to my Lord, I am committed to using whatever ability I have to write and communicate for the best purpose. And no one, not Louis Farrakhan or anyone that may emerge calling to disbelief and misguidance after him, should be judged and considered a Muslim when they clearly fall short of the criteria of the final judge, Allaah.

As we near the end of this brief examination of where Louis Farrakhan fits into Islam in America, 20 years A.E., I want you to read the following excerpts from an interview with Farrakhan. This was printed in a book entitled *American Jihad: Islam After Malcolm X*, which was published nationally in January 1994 and written by Steven Barboza.

Farrakhan's interview was filled (as usual) with distorted beliefs and ideas and concepts that are unquestionably foreign to Islam. I will simply quote a few excerpts of his responses to some of the author's questions to show how far astray he still is. His wording is shrewd and deceptive, and to the ignorant (even among the Muslims) his statements are very dangerous.

20 YEARS A.E. (after Elijah)

Here now is Farrakhan again:

"I BELIEVE THAT I AM DIVINELY CHOSEN. I DON'T SEE ANY WAY THAT I COULD BE SUCCESSFUL WITHOUT GOD'S CHOICE AND BACKING OF ME, ESPECIALLY TO TRY TO ESTABLISH ISLAM IN AMERICA. I THINK THAT ANY OF US THAT STAND UP TODAY ON BEHALF OF ISLAM, ON BEHALF OF TRUTH AND ON BEHALF OF ALLAH-IF WE'RE NOT DIVINELY CHOSEN TO DO THE JOB , WE WON'T BE SUCCESSFUL, AND I BELIEVE THAT I'M DIVINELY CHOSEN AND DIVINELY BACKED BY ALLAH TO BE SUCCESSFUL IN RAISING BLACK PEOPLE UP."

"IF ELIJAH MUHAMMAD BELIEVED HIMSELF TO BE THE MESSENGER OF ALLAH AND ACTED ON THAT BELIEF, WHO CAN JUDGE HIM? CERTAINLY NOT YOU. CERTAINLY NOT ME AND CERTAINLY NOT MALCOLM."

And finally.....

"I WOULDN'T CARE AND DON'T CARE IF NONE OF YOU BELIEVE THAT I AM A MUSLIM. AS I SAID

ISLAM IN AMERICA 1995

TO THOSE 750 IMAMS: TAKE OFF THE ROBES OF ALLAH. THEY DON'T FIT YOU WELL. YOU DON'T KNOW WHO A MUSLIM IS. YOU REALLY DON'T KNOW ANYTHING ABOUT ANYBODY'S ISLAM EXCEPT YOUR OWN. SO WHY DON'T YOU LEAVE THAT TO ALLAH! HE SAYS IN THE QURAN, HE KNOWS BEST WHO ERRS FROM HIS PATH AND KNOWS BEST WHO WALKS ARIGHT. WHY NOT LEAVE THAT TO GOD!

SO I'M A SELF-RESPECTING MAN AND I DON'T FEEL THAT I SHOULD BEND AND SCRAPE TO TRY AND PROVE TO YOU OR THE IMAM OR THE RULERS OF MECCA THAT I AM A MUSLIM. YOU DON'T MAKE ME A MUSLIM. AND SAYING THE THING THAT PLEASES YOU OR MECCA DOESN'T MAKE ME A MUSLIM. I WAS CREATED A MUSLIM BY ALLAH. ISN'T THAT SUFFICIENT?"

Now I ask you, does this sound like a Muslim? This sure sounds like the speech of a munafiq (hypocrite) to me. And surely Allaah knows best!!!

We ask Allaah to increase us in our

20 YEARS A.E. (after Elijah)

deen and help us against the disbelieving people. May He grant us victory against those who disbelieve whether they do it openly, secretly, tacitly or implicitly.

May Allaah give all the wicked leaders such as Farrakhan and the false gods that they worship what they deserve as Allaah has done to those in the past.

And may Allaah enable the Muslims of America and all over the world to not divide into groups and to hold onto that which our leader, Prophet Muhammad (SAAWS) and His companions, our rightly guided forefathers, the real pioneers, held onto.

Allaah's Messenger (SAAWS), in the best guidance, told us in an authentic narration:

"THIS UMMAH WILL DIVIDE INTO 73 SECTS, ALL OF THEM IN THE HELLFIRE EXCEPT ONE." THEY ASKED "AND WHAT IS THAT SECT?" HE SAID "THAT WHICH I AND MY COMPANIONS ARE UPON TODAY".

ISLAM IN AMERICA 1995

May Allaah allow us to live and die upon what he (SAAWS) and his companions were on.

We ask this of Allaah, we repent to Him and we ask Him to forgive us. Ameen.

20 YEARS A.E. (after Elijah)

CHAPTER SEVEN   THE ISLAMIC VIEW OF ELIJAH MUHAMMAD AND THE"NATION OF ISLAM": JUDGING IN LIGHT OF THE QURAN AND THE SUNNAH OF PROPHET MUHAMMAD (SAAWS)

I have to stress from the start that I have very strong views concerning this particular issue. By Allaah having rescued me from the Fire and guided me away from falsehood into truth, I feel compelled to share my opinions on this subject with you. These opinions are supported of course, by the Quran and the Sunnah.

In my humble opinion, one of the most confusing and disturbing aspects of our situation as Muslims in America in 1995, 20 years after Elijah, is the amazing number of people who say that they are Muslims now, (as defined by Allaah and His Messenger, SAAWS), and who also proudly proclaim that they were Muslims during their time in "the Nation of Islam" under Elijah Muhammad! This is an extremely troubling and strange understanding.

ISLAM IN AMERICA 1995

It is a common thing for you to ask someone "How long have you been a Muslim?" and have them reply "I've been a Muslim for forty years". I swear by Allaah, I personally know many brothers and sisters whom I love dearly, for the pleasure of Allaah, and I know for a fact that in 1970 they were followers of Elijah Muhammad.

Their names could have been Harry 2X or Jane 10X, or whatever the case may be. Then, I turn to a recent issue of the *Muslim Journal* and see a photograph of the same brother and his wife, taken at some event, convention or "pioneer dinner" and under the picture it reads "Brother Abdul-Hakim and his wife Sister Jamillah, Muslims for 40 years!

So many times, actually, more than I care to remember, an article appears in this publication about someone from that community who may have achieved something within the community, or maybe even has died and returned to Allaah.

Alhamdulillah, it is a noble thing to acknowledge people among us who have made contributions and

20 YEARS A.E. (after Elijah)

achieved success by Allaah's permission. We should give the appropriate respect to any Muslim while they are living and when they die. But why would anyone still want to render worthless their own good deeds by attaching years and years of believing and following shirk to their Islam?!?

I have to assume the best of the Muslim as we have been commanded to do so. I have to tell myself that this is done solely out of ignorance and no believing Muslim, man or woman would do this intentionally. So, I ask Allaah to guide us all and allow us to form a correct Islamic viewpoint of Elijah Muhammad and the "Nation of Islam".

One of the most important things that we can achieve in this project is providing enough information so that the reader who is sincerely seeking the truth can honestly look at the Islamic view of the teachings of Mr. Muhammad and the "Nation of Islam".

Since the current version of the movement under Louis Farrakhan is simply a continuation or extension of

ISLAM IN AMERICA 1995

the prior legacy, this examination in light of the Quran and Sunnah of Prophet Muhammad (SAAWS) also applies to Farrakhan and his program. This understanding is crucial if we are to truly analyze what has happened since 1975.

Unfortunately, 1995 still finds many people in a perpetual state of denial. 20 years A. E., some of us still can not put the past in its' proper historical perspective Islamically. For anyone who was fortunate enough not to have been around during this time of modern day jahiliya (ignorance), the perception of this movement and its past and present leaders can be very misleading.

Also, there are many Muslims who have immigrated here and they might look at the organizational aspects and the worldly accomplishments of this movement and neglect the fact that **Islamically**, it was built upon falsehood.

To complicate matters even more, one may listen to a man like Farrakhan and his chameleon (with many colors and ever changing) interpretation of this deen and become deluded. Add to

20 YEARS A.E. (after Elijah)

this an endorsement by a respected Muslim personality and one will say "Well, maybe there is still hope." For the purpose of this discussion the focus is on things as they are now, not as we wish they could be.

To the non-Muslim reader or the Muslim reader with an incorrect understanding of Islam, my words may seem harsh and this position might seem extreme. But I want everyone to understand that this issue can not be emphasized enough.

The best way to invite the people to Islam is to clearly explain the basics of what it is based on, using the Quran and the Sunnah as the text, and to clarify, using clear and simple language, what Islam accepts and rejects. This will, inshallah, allow one to see the beauty in the complete way of life that Islam has to offer for all of humanity.

The religion with Allaah, Islam, is easy when properly understood and practiced. It only becomes difficult when one's understanding is tainted with corrupt, distorted and deviant concepts and ideologies. So my words are not harsh at all, and my admonishment is for myself first and then the reader, as my own eyes and ears are closer to me than they are to you.

Let's look at the beautiful words of Allaah in the Quran. This ayat (verse) alone should be enough to summarize the purpose of this chapter and the entire book!

Allah has said (translated):

"IF ANYONE CONTENDS WITH THE MESSENGER EVEN AFTER GUIDANCE HAS BEEN PLAINLY CONVEYED TO HIM AND FOLLOWS A PATH OTHER THAN THAT OF THE BELIEVERS (I.E. THE COMPANIONS), WE SHALL LEAVE HIM IN THE PATH HE HAS CHOSEN AND LAND HIM IN HELL. WHAT AN EVIL REFUGE!

To achieve the objective of this chapter, the focus will primarily be upon the pillars of Islam. These principles are universal and apply to each and every Muslim regardless of ethnicity, national origin or socio-economic status. We will cite each of these pillars of Islam and contrast them with the "5 Principles of Islam"

20 YEARS A.E. (after Elijah)

as taught and practiced by Elijah Muhammad and the "Nation of Islam". This will form the basis for the entire discussion.

The Messenger of Allaah (SAAWS) said in an authentic narration:

"ISLAM IS BUILT ON FIVE: BEARING WITNESS THAT NONE DESERVES TO BE WORSHIPPED AS A DEITY EXCEPT ALLAH, AND THAT MUHAMMAD IS THE MESSENGER OF ALLAAH; ESTABLISHING THE SALAH (PRAYER); GIVING THE ZAKAH (CHARITY); HAJJ (PILGRIMAGE) TO THE HOUSE; AND FASTING RAMADAN".

Now, lets examine the "5 principles of Islam" as taught by the "Nation of Islam. Please bear in mind that even the children in the movement were taught in school to memorize these "principles":

1. TO BELIEVE IN ALLAH AND HIS APOSTLE, THE HONORABLE ELIJAH MUHAMMAD.

2. TO BELIEVE IN PRAYER AT LEAST 5 TIMES A DAY.

3. TO BELIEVE IN GIVING TO THE POOR RATE OR CHARITY.

4. TO BELIEVE IN FASTING, ESPECIALLY DURING THE HOLY MONTH OF RAMADAN.

5. TO BELIEVE IN MAKING THE PILGRIMAGE.

The pillars of Islam are clear and need no explanation. There is so much information in the Quran and the Sunnah to emphasize the importance of these commandments from Allaah. This is the foundation of the deen of Islam.

The principles of "the Nation" are diametrically opposed to Islam beginning with the first point. This principle of shirk and kufr needs no explanation. In the second point, the prayer mentioned here is the prayer according to this movement's understanding, and not the Salah or prayer of Islam. "The Nation's" prayer was standing upright, with your feet at a 45 degree angle and above all, to a false god!

The third principle, giving to the poor rate or charity, was one of "the

20 YEARS A.E. (after Elijah)

Nation's"corrupt forms of zakat that we highlighted in an earlier chapter. This "poor rate" was part of a weekly obligation that one paid and it was the same for everyone regardless of their income or net worth.

The fourth point, fasting, was discussed earlier. And the fifth and final point was also discussed previously. As stated before, making the hajj of the Muslims was not encouraged. It was considered more important and sacred to make the annual Saviour's Day pilgrimage to Chicago every February.

So now, let's ask an important question: If Allaah's Messenger (SAAWS), Al-Amin, Al-Mustafa, the trustworthy one, the chosen one, has said that Islam is based on five and he specified what those five were, what does this tell us about the five principles of the "Nation of Islam"?

How can you build a house without a foundation? Without a doubt, the first principle of this group is enough to nullify any chance of claiming Islam. But because many of us do not understand the true meaning of "La illaha ill Allaah", we won't accept the

ISLAM IN AMERICA 1995

truth enough to hold an Islamically sound position regarding this group.

The evidence is overwhelming and the proof is clear. Falsehood cannot reign where the truth is present. The teachings of Elijah Muhammad with regards to the pillars of iman or faith are well known and have been briefly mentioned earlier. His beliefs and the movement's position on race relations, the Books of Allaah, His Messengers, the Day of Reckoning and the Divine Decree are all well known by us all to be diametrically opposed and against the position of Islam both in the Quran and as practiced by the Messenger of Allaah (SAAWS) and his Companions, may Allaah be pleased with all of them.

It should be clear by now that the Islamic view of Elijah Muhammad, Louis Farrakhan and the "Nation of Islam", both then and now, is that there is no common ground. As hard as it may be for some, it's time to come to grips with reality.

Twenty (20) years is far too long for anyone to still be holding on to this misplaced love and loyalty. A very important and fundamental aspect of

20 YEARS A.E. (after Elijah)

our belief as Muslims is that we love the Messenger of Allaah (SAAWS) more than any other human being. Our leader, Prophet Muhammad (SAAWS) told us in an authentic narration:

"NONE OF YOU CAN BE A PERFECT BELIEVER UNLESS I BECOME MORE DEARER TO HIM THAN HIS FATHER, HIS CHILDREN AND ALL OF THE PEOPLE".

This shows us that Allaah has not made it a requirement of our Islam to forever revere and pay tribute to Elijah Muhammad and the "Nation of Islam". To do this, after Allaah has shined His light on this issue and showed us that the understanding, teachings and practice of this movement are contrary to Islam, is certainly misguidance, error and astray.

While one may argue that the people gained "moral and social benefit" from those teachings, it still doesn't diminish the fact that we have to reject it, Islamically, because it was outside of the realm of Islam, and in the deen of Islam, the end does not

ISLAM IN AMERICA 1995

justify the means. What makes matters even worse is that many attempts were made at giving dawah to Elijah Muhammad in hopes of him attaining an understanding of, accepting and calling his followers to the true Islam.

For what seems to be political reasons, he was allowed to make the Hajj in 1959. He met with many influential Muslims during that time. When he returned to America, he boasted that the whole world of Islam was behind him, and that he was accepted as a brother and leader. Then he resumed with the same programs and teachings that he expoused before his "hajj". In fact, when one examines the chronological course of events, his teachings actually became worse and even further astray!

Even on a local level, within communities all around the country, the members of the "Nation of Islam", particularly the men of the "Fruit of Islam" made it no secret what they thought of "orthodox Muslims".

There was expressed animosity and contempt. They used to refer to the

20 YEARS A.E. (after Elijah)

practicing Muslims as "those spooky Muslims who pray to that mystery god". In fact, a favorite topic of Elijah Muhammad and of many of his most popular ministers of that time was "Who is that Mystery God? In his book, *Message to the Blackman* which I mentioned earlier, he even wrote about this subject in two parts!

We have already cited examples of how people that said things that were clearly Islamically correct, from the Quran and the Sunnah, but against Elijah and "the Nation", were slandered, assaulted and in some cases, even killed. So it should be clear that Elijah Muhammad had a basic understanding of Islam as defined by Allaah, but like all of the false prophets before him, his teachings and actions did not reflect the correct belief.

By far, probably the most popular argument is that the people in America (i.e., the black man) were not in a condition to accept and understand true Islam. It had to be given to them in the manner that it was so that they could be "raised mentally" first. This is the basis for this concept of kufr (disbelief) known as "the first resurrection" which was explained in an earlier chapter. This argument is also one of the most astray.

Why? Because didn't Allaah know what condition the people in America would be in? The condition of the "blackman and woman of America" was certainly in the divine decree of Allaah. It is a fundamental aspect of our aqeedah or belief as Muslims to believe in this decree and accept the good and the bad of it! Could not Allaah have made it permissible for us to use any means necessary and deviate from His Straight Path if He chose to? The Messenger of Allaah (SAAWS) told us in a well known authentic hadith:

"I LEAVE YOU TWO THINGS: THE QURAN AND MY SUNNAH. HOLD ON TO BOTH OF THEM AND YOU WILL NOT GO ASTRAY."

Nowhere does it say that we should hold on to the teachings of Elijah Muhammad, the "lessons", *Message to the Blackman; How to Eat to Live; The Fall of America* or *Our Saviour Has Arrived.* All of these things are misguidance, astray and are clear

20 YEARS A.E. (after Elijah)

examples of "knowledge" that one gains absolutely no benefit from. Even if one does find some "good" in it, the very core and foundation of it is so corrupt that it nullifies any benefit that it claims to offer.

It is because we have openly disobeyed the commandment of Allaah and His Messenger (SAAWS) and have held on to everything except the Quran and the Sunnah that we find ourselves misguided, astray and disunited.

From July 1930 through February 25, 1975, the teachings of Fard Muhammad, and after him, the teachings and practices of Elijah Muhammad and this group known as the "Lost-Found Nation of Islam in America", were deviant, contradictory, opposed to and away from the Straight Path of Allaah and the guidance of His Last Messenger and Seal of the Prophets, Muhammad (SAAWS).

And today, 20 years A. E., in the year 1995 C.E. and 1416 A. H, the "Nation of Islam" is still astray! Anyone that still feels that this is not the truth, then as well as now, they do not have

ISLAM IN AMERICA 1995

the correct understanding of Islam.

As hurtful and discomforting as it may be for some of us, the teachings, concepts and practices of both of these men, from the "old nation" and the "new nation", Elijah Muhammad and Louis Farrakhan, were and are unquestionably and undeniably in contradiction to and outside of Islam.

In concluding this issue of the Islamic view of Elijah Muhammad and the "Nation of Islam", in light of the Quran and the Sunnah of Prophet Muhammad (SAAWS), I ask you to please pay careful attention to the following statements, as they should close the door on this issue once and for all:

Elijah Muhammad lied on Allaah and His Messenger (SAAWS) for over 40 years, and for all those years, he called thousands of people to a path that was clearly not the Straight Path of Allaah.

Allaah has said in the Quran (translated):

"VERILY WHOSOEVER COMMITS SHIRK WITH ALLAAH, ALLAAH

20 YEARS A.E. (after Elijah)

HAS FORBIDDEN PARADISE FOR HIM, AND MADE THE FIRE OF HELL HIS ABODE. THERE WILL BE NO HELPERS FOR THE WRONGDOERS".

The Messenger of Allaah (SAAWS) said in an authentic narration:

"ANYONE WHO MEETS ALLAAH (DIES) WHILE DOING SHIRK, HE WILL ENTER THE FIRE OF HELL!"

Thus are the words of Allaah and His Messenger (SAAWS), the best and only acceptable and irrefutable evidence and guidance upon which to form any Islamic viewpoint.

And if Elijah Muhammad died on what he taught thousands of people for over 40 years, then he died the death of a disbeliever. Sad but true. And this is not from my own opinion. The evidence has been presented, the proofs were presented, and the evidence found in the Quran and the Sunnah are in overwhelming abundance! And Allaah shall render the final verdict.

Imam Malik, may Allaah have mercy on him made a very profound statement and it certainly applies to this issue:

What was Islam then is Islam now and what was not Islam then is not Islam now!

I ask Allaah to allow us all to judge anyone calling to Islam by the Quran and the Sunnah of His Messenger (SAAWS) and that we have the courage to speak a word of truth, even if it be against our ownselves. As Allaah has said in the Quran (translated):

"OH YE WHO BELIEVE! KEEP YOUR DUTY TO ALLAAH AND FEAR HIM, AND ALWAYS SPEAK THE TRUTH. HE WILL DIRECT YOU TO RIGHTEOUS DEEDS AND WILL FORGIVE YOU YOUR SINS. WHOSOEVER OBEYS ALLAAH AND HIS MESSENGER HAS INDEED ATTAINED A GREAT ACHIEVEMENT."

May Allaah allow us to act on His commandments and to implement them in each and every aspect of our lives. I ask this of Him for myself and all the believers, and I ask Him to forgive us all. Ameen.

20 YEARS A.E. (after Elijah)

CHAPTER EIGHT "MUSLIM AMERICAN SPOKESMAN FOR HUMAN SALVATION": THE MINISTRY OF IMAM W. DEEN MOHAMMED.....A CLOSE EXAMINATION

Entering into the 1990's, there was a re-emergence of an organized group under the leadership of Imam W. Deen Mohammed, formerly known as Wallace D. Muhammad and W.D. Muhammad. He officially changed the spelling of his last name from the way that the Prophet Muhammad (SAAWS) spelled it, to the spelling which he said was used on his birth certificate.

What is astounding about this fact is that after Imam Mohammed changed the spelling of his name, many of his followers who had the last name "Muhammad" changed to spelling of their names to resemble his. Moreover, even some of the masjids that were named "Masjid Muhammad" changed the spelling to "Masjid Mohammed". One would think that every one from this community suddenly "discovered" that their birth certificates were wrong and they had to change them.

ISLAM IN AMERICA 1995

For sure, I have no problems with a healthy and sincere respect for leadership, but this type of behavior defines blind following to the highest degree. Please read chapter nine (9) of this book for a brief discussion of blind following, as it has many facets and characteristics.

In the early 1990's, we began to see more of an active effort by Imam Mohammed in terms of the dawah or propagation effort in America. He formed "The Ministry of Imam W. Deen Mohammed". He began traveling extensively throughout the country and to various other parts of the world, talking about Islam as he understands it. It was around this time that he began being referred to as "The Muslim American Spokesman for Human Salvation".

One thing that I've never understood is this fixation with always having some official title. This phenomenon seems particularly present within the African-American communities, both Muslim and non-Muslim. In this new title lies the foundation for the entire dawah effort of Imam Mohammed and the Imams across the country that support his leadership.

20 YEARS A.E. (after Elijah)

Any effort to educate people about Islam and the Muslims has to be considered as a good thing. There is a great need for the dawah in America to become more organized and more structured. Any attempt made to this end should be looked at in a positive light.

The problem occurs, however, when the core methodology of any propagation effort differs from the methodology of the best of those who gave dawah, Prophet Muhammad (SAAWS). When the approach to calling the people to Islam starts to bear less and less resemblance to the approach of the Prophet (SAAWS) and his Companions, our rightly guided predecessors, it is time to take a real close look and thoroughly examine our program.

Such a problem exists with the ministry of Imam W. Deen Mohammed. One might say that because of the time that we are living in, we have to use a different methodology to reach a different people. To this I say that the actual techniques may vary, of course, within the bounds that Allaah and His Messenger (SAAWS) have set for

ISLAM IN AMERICA 1995

us. But the core methodology, the language and interpretation of the Quran and the Sunnah is a constant and never changes!

There are many similarities and clear parallels from which to draw more than enough clear examples. The Messenger of Allaah (SAAWS) developed solid communication and mutual respect with the people in the land who were not believers. But he never altered his message simply to make it more pleasing to the people. He simply conveyed in the best of manners what Allaah had commanded him to convey.

Allaah's Messenger, in stressing the importance of one's actions being related to his intentions, He (SAAWS) said:

"ACTIONS ARE BUT BY INTENTIONS AND THERE IS FOR EVERY PERSON ONLY THAT WHICH HE INTENDED. SO HE WHOSE MIGRATION WAS FOR ALLAAH AND HIS MESSENGER, THEN HIS MIGRATION WAS FOR ALLAAH AND HIS MESSENGER, AND HE WHOSE MIGRATION WAS TO ATTAIN SOME WORLDLY GOAL

20 YEARS A.E. (after Elijah)

OR TO TAKE A WOMAN IN MARRIAGE, THEN HIS MIGRATION WAS FOR THAT WHICH HE MIGRATED."

In this hadith, we find many great benefits and lessons. When we do things sincerely for Allaah and stay within the guidelines that Allaah and His Messenger (SAAWS) have set forth, the success is assured. Whenever we begin to conform our programs, including our dawah, to what is simply pleasing to the people, all we gain is the pleasure of those people, and we sacrifice the pleasure of Allaah!

In this brief chapter, I will give a few examples of how the current dawah effort does not reflect the correct dawah that the Muslim has been commanded to give. Let's begin by giving the beautiful hadith of the Messenger of Allaah (SAAWS) where he sent one of his companions, Mu'aadh (may Allah be pleased with him) to Yemen. He (SAAWS) said to Mu'aadh:

"YOU ARE GOING TO A NATION FROM THE PEOPLE OF THE BOOK, SO LET THE FIRST THING

THAT YOU CALL THEM TO BE THAT THEY SHOULD MAKE ALL WORSHIP SOLELY FOR ALLAAH, THE MOST HIGH. SO IF THEY REALIZE THAT, THEN INFORM THEM THAT ALLAAH HAS OBLIGATED UPON THEM FIVE PRAYERS IN THE DAY AND NIGHT. IF THEY PRAY THEM INFORM THEM THAT ALLAAH HAS OBLIGATED UPON THEM ZAKAT FROM THEIR WEALTH - TO BE TAKEN FROM THEIR RICH AND GIVEN TO THEIR POOR. IF THEY ACCEPT THAT, THEN TAKE IT FROM THEM, BUT AVOID THE BEST PART OF THE PEOPLE'S PROPERTY".

This hadith is jammed packed with wisdom, and it conveys perfectly the type of dawah that the caller to Islam should present to the people, whether they be Christian, Jew or whatever. Notice how the Messenger of Allaah (SAAWS), who Allaah has said that in him we have the perfect example, he didn't come with a watered down, conciliatory message aimed at pleasing anyone. He wasn't offensive in his speech, yet he still clearly conveyed the truth. I used this

20 YEARS A.E. (after Elijah)

particular hadith first because it clearly contradicts the approach that we find popular today.

I am reading a pamphlet which is currently among those being distributed by W. Deen Mohammed Publications. It is entitled *Religion is Sincerity (Religion means to realign your life)*. It is subtitled *Clarifying Misconceptions*. In this fold out styled pamphlet, which consists of 5 pages, not once do the words "Allaah" or "Prophet Muhammad" appear. The pamphlet specifically opens with "With the Name of God, the Merciful Benefactor, the Merciful Redeemer."

How can any Muslim, let alone a Muslim leader with worldwide recognition, write an entire "dawah" pamphlet and not once mention Allaah or His Messenger (SAAWS)? "God" is used exclusively throughout this pamphlet, and I've noticed in the public speeches of Imam Mohammed and many of the Imam's within his ministry, they tend to use this non specific approach.

The Christians have no problem coming to us in the name of Jesus, why do we have so much trouble

ISLAM IN AMERICA 1995

calling on Allaah by His proper name and giving our leader, Prophet Muhammad (SAAWS) his just due and the respect that he deserves? This ministry has the audacity to go before the United States Senate and give the opening invocation and ask for "God's blessing" on the United States of America, the (then) President Bush and all of these other personalities, but will not go to them with what Allaah has commanded.

We can sit with all types of people; Christian preachers, Jewish rabbis, Buddhists, all sorts of people, and discuss the commonality of all the major faiths, and conduct these endless "interfaith dialogues". But ask someone from among the people who support this ministry, even the Imams to sit with you to discuss the Quran or the understanding of an authentic hadith or other aspects of the Sunnah, and they arrogantly refuse. It is clear that this type of propagation sends more mixed signals and confuses more people than it helps.

The ministry of Imam W. Deen Mohammed does Islam, as well as the people of America, a great

20 YEARS A.E. (after Elijah)

disservice when it does not convey the beautiful message of Islam in it's essence. For sure, the people among the pagan Arabs, who used to dance naked around the Kabaa and commit all types of shirk and other atrocities in jahiliya (ignorance), fully accepted the message of Islam without a watered down version. If they could accept this, then the people of America with their "higher intellect" can certainly be given the clear undiluted message of Islam, based on the Quran and the Sunnah, and they will embrace it and grow in it, if Allaah so pleases.

My analysis of the ministry of Imam W. Deen Mohammed is that while it is gaining some media exposure for Islam and the Muslim life in this country, at what price is this being achieved? Do we have to go so far as to extol the virtues of the Constitution and compare it to the Shariah (Islamic law) as Imam Mohammed did in his book, "Al-Islam, Unity and Leadership?"

This is not an isolated example. As of this writing, Spring 1995, Imam W. Deen Mohammed still continues to give tafseer (commentary, explanation, etc.) of the Quran, explain things about Islam without having any basis in the Quran and the Sunnah of the Messenger of Allaah (SAAWS) and use concepts that are clearly innovated ideas.

The examples are too numerous to mention here, and they could (and may have to become) the topic of another book. However, I will give one glaring example. This comment is taken from the May 19, 1995 issue of the *Muslim Journal*. This is from his weekly centerfold column which appears in this newspaper. This article was taken from one of his public addresses where he was commenting on "the conduct of war" and he made the following statement:

"I've heard so many Muslim preachers preaching about Islam is going to be the dominant religion and they are trying to excite all of us to stand upon that. They say Islam must dominate on this Earth and that the Muslim nations must dominate non-Muslim nations. They say that Islam must replace all other religions. **That's incorrect.** I don't have to say that to these scholars, they know that

20 YEARS A.E. (after Elijah)

it's incorrect".

This is in clear contradiction to the numerous ayats of the Quran and the authentic hadiths where Allaah and His Messenger (SAAWS) have said that Islam is the religion with Allaah and that Allaah has chosen Islam as the perfect deen (way of life) and the example of Prophet Muhammad (SAAWS) as the perfect example for all of humanity. This is just one example of the dawah of the ministry of Imam W. Deen Muhammad! For further examples, just pick up any copy of *Muslim Journal* any week and carefully examine for yourself.

Just how much further will we continue to dwell down the path to our own destruction? Do we continue to give events where the men and women, Muslim and non-Muslim, sit next to one another and intermingle, clearly defying the commandments of Allaah and His Messenger (SAAWS)? Do we continue to let Islamically ignorant Imams justify this by saying that this promotes "unity" and that the separation of men and women in the masjid is a foreign concept that was brought to us incorrectly by Fard

ISLAM IN AMERICA 1995

Muhammad?!? What kind of unity is being achieved in disobedience to Allaah?

Will we continue to frequent the masjids that support this ministry and watch our sisters parade around in improper clothing, wearing perfume and makeup, all because "the Imam" said that this is O.K.? Muslim brothers and sisters, it is time to come correct and stop this foolishness. We are only hastening our own ruin.

These are the kinds of community concerns that must be addressed by the ministry of W. Deen Mohammed before it can even begin to go among the non-Muslims and invite the people to Islam. Let us begin to make the criteria for leadership in America a solid understanding of the Quran and Sunnah, combined with a good moral character, and stop this popularity contest of leadership based on national or ethnic origin, who you're related to or who has the biggest following!

Now, as to add validity to the practice of bidaa' or innovation, there is this attempt to establish a new madhhab, or school of thought in America. I am

20 YEARS A.E. (after Elijah)

not going to elaborate on this issue too much, as I am still in the process of researching all of the facts surrounding this issue. In the coming months, inshallah, I will be presenting my findings in the form of a journal.

For now, I'll simply say that we as Muslims haven't even begun to apply hardly any of the thousands of authentic narration's, the hadiths of Allaah's Messenger (SAAWS). Why do we need to develop a new school of thought and we haven't even begun to properly implement the guidance from that best "school", the one that Allaah said was the perfect example to emulate, study and pattern our affairs after?

I just pray Allaah that anyone who sits on this "National Fiqh Committee," that has been established as a consultative group to help develop this new madhhab, they take account of the entire concept of establishing a madhhab. Some from among this group have enough of a basic understanding of the Quran and the Sunnah and they know that this is not a recommended or a necessary thing.

ISLAM IN AMERICA 1995

More good can be done, the Muslims of America and the people of the American society will be much better served if the ministry of Imam W. Deen Mohammed would commit itself to reviving that real pioneering spirit that the companions of Allaah's Messenger (SAAWS) had instead of trying to find a way to validate things that have no basis in this deen as the Messenger of Allaah (SAAWS) and his companions taught, understood and practiced it. And Allaah knows best.

Do we have to encourage the Muslims to march in parades celebrating their "cultural and human excellence"? Do we continue to justify these things by lying on the Messenger of Allaah (SAAWS) and using a forged hadith, as Imam Mohammed did in a June 28, 1991 article in the *Muslim Journal* where he said:

"The Prophet said "See that when you go among other people that you don't compromise their culture". Where did this "narration" come from?!? This type of thing carries over into the understanding and speech of many of the people and some of the Imams from within this ministry. I recently read a book by one of the so-called

20 YEARS A.E. (after Elijah)

"knowledgeable" (but clearly ignorant) people that supports Imam Mohammed.

This brother, Mustafa El-Amin, an author and lecturer, who has been given the title of Imam (in an article in the *Muslim Journal*), though I know of no masjid or any jammah (group) that he is responsible for, wrote a book in which he used three (3) forged hadith in a row, in one statement! We as Muslims know them all; "Seek knowledge, even if it is as far as China", "Seek knowledge from the cradle to the grave", and these other tales attributed to Allaah's Messenger (SAAWS).

For sure, we have a long, long way to go before our dawah compares to the dawah of the Messenger of Allaah (SAAWS) and his companions. Once we begin to do this, Allaah will allow us to see the people embrace Islam in it's entirety. We can't be allured and deluded by big numbers today. 15,000 at a convention in Washington, D.C., or 10,000 at this event, etc. We see throughout the history of Islam that the masses of people were never on the straight path at the same time.

ISLAM IN AMERICA 1995

Once we begin to really call to Islam in this country, then the masses of people will really gain a great benefit. It is this type of effort that truly represents leadership, and is truly worthy of being followed. This type of leadership was and still is exemplified by the best example for mankind, the Messenger sent to all nations, Prophet Muhammad ibn Abdullah, may the peace and blessings of Allaah be upon him, the **true** Muslim spokesman for Human Salvation. Why? Because Allaah said he is!

20 YEARS A.E. (after Elijah)

CHAPTER NINE A REFUTATION OF ALL BLIND FOLLOWING: REFER IT BACK TO ALLAAH AND HIS MESSENGER!!!

As one can clearly see, there is a great danger in blindly following anyone, from the past or present, especially if what they are calling or leading the people to is other than what Allaah and His Messenger (SAAWS) have given us.

This issue of blind following is not referring solely to following deviant or astray ideologies, but it also includes following those people who are seemingly on the straight path and are calling the people to Islam, the Quran and the Sunnah. However, when one carefully examines their speech, it is a great deal of their own personal opinion and often times is articulated as if it was from the Quran and the Sunnah.

My reason for mentioning both of these types of blind following is that often times, in our search of knowledge and truth, the new convert (or revert) to Islam, or those of us that are now more actively seeking to correctly practice this deen, we are

ISLAM IN AMERICA 1995

easily led into extremes.

One can listen to a person and because he sounds, acts or even looks as if he is on the truth, we blindly follow this person and make this person above question and beyond reproach. We might hear something, a statement or a particular position expressed, and instead of seeking the origin and correctness of these things from the Quran and the authentic Sunnah, we automatically assume that if **this** person said it, it has to be totally correct.

For certain, there has to be a certain level of trust between the student and the teacher, and the Imam or Shaikh and the "follower". When it comes to the basic and fundamental things in the Quran and the Sunnah, most questions are unnecessary questions, except for the new Muslim or one who may be simply seeking clarity or a better understanding of these fundamentals.

The kind of blind following that I am referring to here specifically, is the following of the practices, opinions and the personal positions that one may express, that have no basis in

20 YEARS A.E. (after Elijah)

the Quran or the Sunnah.

Moreover, often times when an Imam from among us or a "student of knowledge" who has been entrusted with the responsibility of educating the people (teaching classes, counseling, etc.) may make a statement, that may reflect what he may have derived from the Quran and Sunnah based on his understanding.

While we all know the hadiths which speak of the merits of a scholar, many of these people will readily admit (sometimes) that they do not possess anything near this level of scholarship. Yet, many people act as if when these issues or positions are expressed, they are binding and obligatory upon the people, students or followers. At times, it goes to such an extreme, one begins to think and act as if Allaah and His Messenger (SAAWS) commanded us to follow these individuals and their groups.

Anyone who comes in contact with the discussions of those among the blind followers will no doubt agree that this is one of the major causes of the decline of the Muslims and is a

ISLAM IN AMERICA 1995

reason for our sometimes backwards ways. This blind following has transformed the minds of many among us so much, that they do not think except with the minds of other people. It is a common thing for someone to come to you and begin expressing what they have learned or acquired, and instead of saying that "Allaah said" or "the Messenger of Allaah (SAAWS) said", they'll say "Abdullah said" or "the Shaikh said" or "the Imam said" such and such.

Many times, this is not the fault of the teacher, Shaikh, Imam or student of knowledge. Any sincere person from among these categories will always make it a practice to preface their talks, discussions and statements with "Allaah said" and "the Messenger of Allaah (SAAWS) said", etc.

This clearly separates what one is expressing from the Quran and the Sunnah from what is their own personal position and opinion. While often times, the personal opinion or position may be found to be correct, it is still not of the same importance as a commandment from Allaah or the Prophet Muhammad (SAAWS).

20 YEARS A.E. (after Elijah)

The only person whose opinion can not be argued or refuted on any issue is the Last Messenger of Allaah (SAAWS), because Allaah has said to us in the Quran (translated):

"NOR DOES HE (MUHAMMAD) SPEAK OF HIS OWN DESIRE. IT IS NO LESS THAN REVELATION SENT DOWN TO HIM"

No one from among us can truthfully make that claim. Contrary to some of the things that we've heard various personalities from among us say at times, no one's feelings or personal experiences can make their position correct when their position is contrary to that of the Quran and the Sunnah.

Allaah tells us in the Quran (translated):

"MANKIND WERE ONE COMMUNITY AND ALLAAH SENT PROPHETS WITH GLAD TIDINGS AND WARNINGS AND WITH THEM HE SENT THE BOOK IN TRUTH, TO JUDGE BETWEEN PEOPLE IN MATTERS WHEREIN THEY DIFFER."

After reading this clear

commandment from Allaah, where does one still find room for blindly following anyone apart from Allaah's Messenger (SAAWS)? This is clearly not from Islam and anyone who does this after being directed to the correct way, he is ignorant and astray.

Another very important point needs to be made here. This blind following is not limited to any one specific community. This is present among various communities, in various places throughout the country. It exists under the direction and "leadership" of numerous Imams, Shaikhs and other people who are responsible for leading groups of people. And blind following also happens among various levels of Islamically "knowledgeable" people.

There are individuals who are well informed with regards to matters of this deen, and they clearly know the difference between Sunnah and bidaa', iman and kufr, and deviance and following the straight way. Yet, they still allow themselves to fall victim to blind following.

One simply has to travel around the country and visit various Muslim

20 YEARS A.E. (after Elijah)

communities and this will become crystal clear. In some places, all one needs to do is put on a white thaub (long, robelike garment), speak halfway decent Arabic, seem to understand Islam, use some Islamic terminology, (inshallah, mashallah, subhanallah), then add, as icing on the cake, an unheard of, authentic (or unauthentic) hadith, and he's "in like that", complete with a throng of loyal followers!

It is sad that 20 years A.E., after Elijah, we still haven't learned our lesson when it comes to blind following. This applies to those that were part of the "Nation of Islam", as well as those who were not. They too, have exhibited this vulnerability to blindly following men. Islam is a single deen, and there are no madhhabs or ways that one is obligated to follow except for the way of The Messenger of Allaah (SAAWS) and his guidance.

Allaah said in the Quran (translated):

"SAY (O MUHAMMAD): THIS IS MY WAY; I INVITE UNTO ALLAAH, WITH SURE KNOWLEDGE. I AND WHOSOEVER FOLLOWS ME ALSO

ISLAM IN AMERICA 1995

MUST INVITE OTHERS TO ALLAAH WITH SURE KNOWLEDGE. GLORIFIED AND EXALTED BE ALLAAH. I AM NOT OF MUSHRIKEEN (THOSE WHO WORSHIP OTHERS ALONG WITH ALLAAH).

None of the scholars, including the four Imams of the popular schools of thought, Imams Abu Haneefah, Maalik, Ahmad and ash-Shaafi'ee, ever ordered the people to follow them in their opinions. They enjoined on their students to take from where they took from, and they all agreed that if anyone found an authentic hadith, that is their madhhab!

They all warned the people against blind following. It was only the later generations who created new madhhabs and ascribed them to the original Imams. They are the ones who made this blind following of the opinions of the madhhabs appear as if they were binding upon the people.

We find this same thing today. It is even common to see people do things, some of which are beneficial and good things that are actually part of the Sunnah, and when you ask them why

20 YEARS A.E. (after Elijah)

they do these things, they'll simply reply that everyone is doing it, or Imam so and so, or Shaikh so and so said to do this. This, for sure, is a form of blind following.

As Muslims, we are commanded to know and understand as much of the Sunnah as we can. When Allaah commands us to do a thing, we do it, without question or hesitation. This and blind following are certainly not equal! No Imam, scholar or Shaikh from before our time or of our time is to be obeyed or followed unquestionably.

Look at what one of the companions of the Messenger of Allaah (SAAWS), Adee ibn Haatim said:

"I HEARD ALLAAH'S MESSENGER (SAWS) RECITE: "THEY (JEWS AND CHRISTIANS) TOOK THEIR RABBIS AND THEIR MONKS TO BE THEIR LORDS BESIDES ALLAAH."

"SO I SAID: OH MESSENGER OF ALLAAH, THEY DID NOT WORSHIP THEM. SO HE (SAWS) SAID, "VERILY IF THEY MADE SOMETHING PERMISSIBLE FOR

ISLAM IN AMERICA 1995

THEM, THEN THEY MADE IT PERMISSIBLE AND IF THEY MADE SOMETHING FORBIDDEN TO THEM, THEN THEY MADE IT FORBIDDEN - THAT IS THEIR WORSHIP OF THEM."

This is exemplary of what we see today in too many instances, some of which I mentioned previously, and some that I will mention in the forthcoming chapter.

My advice, especially to the new Muslim or the non-Muslim that reads this book, and I hope that it is clearly understood:

Blindly following someone, or pledging undying loyalty or devotion to a particular group or individual, is NOT a requirement in Islam.

You do not have to belong to a national group which a specific number of members in order to be considered a Muslim. The greatest Imam is the Messenger of Allaah, Prophet Muhammad (SAAWS), and he is the only one that we are commanded to follow as Muslims.

For sure, we don't want anyone to

20 YEARS A.E. (after Elijah)

think that we are a people without organization, and who don't support leadership. But there is no priesthood in Islam, no one has a direct line to Allaah and there is no one from among us receiving any revelation.

Once this is understood, you will never become a victim of blind following, and you will be well on your way towards really understanding the meaning of "La illaha il allaah, Muhammadur Rasullullah". Nothing deserves to be worshipped as a deity except Allaah and Muhammad (SAAWS) is the Messenger of Allaah. There is no comparison between this and blind following. The choice is clear.

May Allaah protect the innocent people from the dangers and misguidance of blind following, and may He give us all the courage and conviction to do as He has commanded in the Quran (translated):

"IN MATTERS WHEREIN YOU DIFFER, REFER IT BACK TO ALLAAH AND HIS MESSENGER".

ISLAM IN AMERICA 1995

CHAPTER TEN WHERE DO WE GO FROM HERE?: A BRIEF LOOK AT THE CURRENT STATE OF THE MUSLIM UMMAH IN AMERICA

After reading this book, one may wonder whether there is any hope for the continued development and success of the Muslims in America. I do not want anyone to complete this book and feel that all is lost. In spite of the many trials and setbacks that Allaah has allowed us to experience over the past 20 years, there are many bright spots and positives as we move through this year, 1995 and inshallah, look ahead to the future, if Allaah wills for us to still be in existence.

Allaah has told us in the Quran (translated):

"SURELY THE BELIEVERS WILL WIN THROUGH".

As Muslims and believers in Allaah, we put our trust and faith solely in Allaah. As long as we have the courage and the conviction to change what is in our hearts, Allaah has said that He will change our condition, and He has assured us success and

20 YEARS A.E. (after Elijah)

victory in our struggle to practice this deen, Islam. One can clearly see the evidence of this as you travel across this country. Within various cities in America, there is a growing number of Muslims who have committed themselves to the spread of Islam in its correct form, free and clear of deviation and innovation.

Here on the East Coast, we are fortunate enough to have among us those who are dedicated to gaining a better understanding of our way of life, and projecting this understanding to the American public.

We are beginning to rediscover the authentic sources of Islamic information, and we are beginning to utilize these sources, thus improving our understanding of Islam, based upon the Quran and the Sunnah of the Prophet Muhammad (SAAWS). This is enabling the sincere Muslims to correct our ways of error of the past, and to move completely away from the things that we did, both knowingly and unknowingly, during our various stages of ignorance.

The dawah or propagation effort is

ISLAM IN AMERICA 1995

becoming more prolific in America. This growth needs to be sustained in order for us to fulfill our responsibility of carrying the beautiful message of Islam to the masses. Inshallah, in the very near future, more progress will be made towards developing and organizing this effort. Those in the forefront of this effort will be the individuals that are calling to the correct understanding and practice of Islam in its entirety.

More and more of the authentic and classic works of Islam are being translated into English and being made available to the masses of people in America for the first time. Very recently, a more accurate English translation of the Quran has been completed and made available throughout America.

The Interpretation of the Meanings of the Noble Quran in the English Language is a beautiful work that allows the English speaking reader to gain a more correct meaning of the Quran and it uses only the authentic narration's of the Messenger of Allaah (SAAWS) in explaining the verses.

20 YEARS A.E. (after Elijah)

These self proclaimed "scholars", or "knowledgeable people, with their poor, incomplete (and in some cases, non-existent) understanding of the Arabic language (not to mention of the science of hadith and sound Islamic knowledge in general) who criticize and reject this excellent translation do not even merit consideration here. Their ignorance is of an even higher level, but their influence is dangerous nonetheless.

More importantly, on an individual level, Muslims are making more of an effort to learn the language of the Quran, the Arabic language, so that we can begin to comprehend the message and guidance of the Quran and the Sunnah. This will also enable us to gain the ability to safeguard ourselves from people who are determined to interpret the book of Allaah using their own (usually wrong) opinions!

As we begin a more thorough examination of the Sunnah of the Prophet Muhammad (SAAWS), it will become crystal clear that this guidance is loaded with practical examples for us to apply to our situation here in 1995, and to

ISLAM IN AMERICA 1995

implement in our daily lives in the future.

Contrary to the expressed opinions of some individuals, personalities and groups among us, there is absolutely no need for us to invent or discover "new" ways or "modern" methodologies that seem to address our situation today in America. This position is unquestionably an Islamically incorrect position and as we have seen, it opens the floodgates of deviance and innovation. The Messenger of Allaah (SAAWS) said to us in a well known authentic narration:

"THE WORST OF ALL THINGS IN THIS DEEN ARE NEWLY INVENTED MATTERS, FOR EVERY NEWLY INVENTED MATTER IS AN INNOVATION, EVERY INNOVATION IS ASTRAY AND EVERY ASTRAY IS IN THE HELLFIRE."

For one to state that there is a need for new ways of doing things is to imply that Allaah did not know what reality we would be confronted with today in America 1995! If one would simply reflect on the thousands of authentic narration's from our leader,

20 YEARS A.E. (after Elijah)

Prophet Muhammad (SAAWS), not to mention the thousands of verses in the Quran, you will see that the guidance and perfect example contained in this truth forecast exactly what the current state of the Muslim Ummah in America is today! So, Islam does not need a revision or a revival. Our understanding, implementation and practice of Islam as given to us in the Quran and the Sunnah needs to be revived!!!

What is really needed in my opinion, based on my experience and struggles within the Muslim community in America, is a greater emphasis on community and economic development. Alhamdulillah, this is beginning to happen in various places throughout the country.

After beginning the process of gaining a better understanding of Islam, it becomes an obligation to use what is allowable and lawful in Islam to strengthen our collective situations in our personal and community affairs. There are groups of intelligent individuals whom Allaah has blessed to develop a solid, fundamental knowledge of Islam, and they are using this acquired, beneficial

ISLAM IN AMERICA 1995

knowledge for the improvement of the Muslims at large.

Muslims are beginning to purchase property; masajid, schools, businesses, etc. that are owned solely by the Muslims and acquired and financed interest free. It is irrefutable that ribaa' or interest is unlawful in Islam in all forms. Instead of using the institution of interest as an excuse not to build or acquire anything, Muslims are starting to take action and develop real, practical solutions and strategies.

Allaah has blessed the sincere, thinking Muslim with the vision to find Islamically acceptable methods of financing property and acquiring other types of wealth that can be used for the benefit of the people. This is genuinely a blessing from Allaah, especially since the Muslims as a whole have neglected and in most cases abandoned the institution of Zakat!

I have to acknowledge the efforts of many of the Muslims who immigrated to America from various places around the world. Many of them have done as the companions of the

20 YEARS A.E. (after Elijah)

Messenger of Allaah (SAAWS), our rightly guided forefathers did.

They sacrificed, lived modest lifestyles and pooled their resources in order to attain the necessary wealth and property needed to establish the Muslim community life. Among the indigenous, American born Muslims, especially the "African American" Muslims, this type of collective effort is just now beginning to become a reality.

Many of us are still plagued with the disease of not trusting anyone that looks like us, and we still look for support and assistance from everyone and everywhere else. As one brother said to me once, we buy what we want and beg for what we need. May Allaah cure us of this pettiness and instill in us a greater trust of one another based on Islam and not some ethnic or national origin.

For certain, those among us that Allaah has blessed to have this vision, they should be supported and they have a prominent role to play in the future of the Muslim Ummah in America if we are to be successful in establishing community life here. And Allaah knows best.

The Messenger of Allaah (SAAWS) said to us in an authentic narration:

"THE BEST OF YOU IN JAHILIYA (IGNORANCE) ARE THE BEST OF YOU IN DEEN (ISLAM), PROVIDED THAT HE HAS AN UNDERSTANDING OF THE DEEN (ISLAM)."

This has been proven to be true, time and time again.

There is another very important issue that relates to the current status of the Muslim ummah in America. **Please read this very carefully.** The Messenger of Allaah (SAAWS) has commanded the believers, his Ummah, the Muslims, to take the middle course. This is clearly his Sunnah.

And he has said in an authentic narration:

"WHOEVER TURNS AWAY FROM MY SUNNAH IS NOT OF ME".

As Muslims, we should never go to one extreme or the other. This applies to our personal lives as well as our

20 YEARS A.E. (after Elijah)

spiritual lives, with regards to matters of worship. Today, the concept of "extremism" is very prevalent and it has manifested itself in some very dangerous ways. I want to make it clear that when I refer to "extremism" I am not referring to this distorted view of what constitutes extremism that we see reflected by the popular western media.

To give an example of what I am specifically referring to, I offer this real scenario:

In one corner, you have Muslims who see nothing wrong whatsoever with attending and even sponsoring events where Muslims, Christians and Jews all come together, singing gospel songs, intermingling freely, men and women even shaking hands and embracing each other. They listen to these people who in one breath talk about the "common bond" between the three faiths, and then make statements of clear shirk when referring to their false lords other than Allaah!

The Muslims who engage in this "interfaith" dialogue will not stop to think for one moment about giving

ISLAM IN AMERICA 1995

these people the correct dawah and inviting them to Islam in the proper manner. This will make it appear to the uninformed person that there are no real differences between the belief systems and practices of Islam, Christianity and Judaism. So one may ask "why should I become a Muslim and believe in Allaah when we are all one big, happy, HUMAN family?!

Do not these Muslims realize what Allaah and His Messenger (SAAWS) have said about this type of mentality and the dangers and misguidance that lie within it? The verses of the Quran that mention in detail how the Jews and Christians will never be satisfied until they turn you away from your deen are clear proof of how this approach is definitely an extreme course of action.

In the other corner, you have those Muslims who advocate the development and training of an army to overthrow the American government. Here we can't even use the clear guidance of Allaah and His Messenger (SAAWS) to unify on such issues as the sighting of the moon for Ramadan, etc., but we can think of

20 YEARS A.E. (after Elijah)

uniting to overthrow the government!

Most of these people haven't invested any substantial time in the dawah effort in this country, and in most cases, their understanding of Islam is tainted with all sorts of deviant and misguided philosophies. Yet, they would actually like to set up little militias, training camps throughout America, with the agenda and dream of taking over America.

The Muslims from this corner have an understanding of Islam that is so astray that they would advocate, support, and even participate in the bombing of a building like the World Trade Center! They don't even stop to think about the sin of killing innocent people, let alone harming or **killing the HUNDREDS of Muslims**, sincere, practicing Muslims who go to work in that building each day to support their families, contribute within the community and fulfill their responsibilities!

Both of these two extremes are outside of what is lawful and permissible in Islam, and they certainly do not reflect the guidance of the Quran and the Sunnah. These

ISLAM IN AMERICA 1995

issues greatly impact the Muslim Ummah in a negative way. For us to develop in this country, we must go back to basics and take the middle course.

But in the face of all of the obstacles, the outlook for the Muslim Ummah in America, in my assessment, is positive and looking better each day. Why? Because unlike the times prior to 1975, and the days that have gone by over the past 20 years, there is a light shining brightly in America. Allaah is allowing the masses of people in this country to begin to see the light of the Quran and the authentic Sunnah of His last and greatest Messenger, Prophet Muhammad (SAAWS).

His light and guidance has come after a time when there was darkness, with no correct guidance. The presence of this light in the lives of the Muslim Ummah in America has extinguished the fire of falsehood, based upon shirk, misguidance, deviation and innovation.

The truth is clearly shining brighter than ever before in America. As long as we hold fast to the dictates of

20 YEARS A.E. (after Elijah)

Islam based on the Quran and the Sunnah, and reinforce this with a plan of action based on what is lawful in Islam, the success and the victory is ours for the taking. We have been promised this by Allaah. And surely Allaah's promise is true!

May Allaah allow His light to shine on the Muslim Ummah in America and all over the world until the Day of Judgment. Ameen.

ISLAM IN AMERICA 1995

SUMMARY AND CLOSING THOUGHTS

My intention when beginning this project was to give an overview of the events, personalities and situations that have impacted the Muslims and the religion of Islam in America since 1975.

In order to accomplish this, it was essential to provide the reader, both the Muslim and non-Muslim, with a background on the group which for years was identified erroneously as the representative body of Muslims and Islam in this country.

The movement known as the "Lost-Found Nation of Islam in America" has a long and detailed history. What I've tried to do is give a brief history of the origin of this group, discuss it's past and current leaders and their ideologies and programs, and highlight some of the key events that occurred during the time of Elijah Muhammad up until 1975 and Louis Farrakhan from 1978 through the present.

I realize that some of the information may have been read or heard before

20 YEARS A.E. (after Elijah)

by some. To many people, some of the information and events discussed in this book may have been their very first contact with this information.

There has always been, and there still exists, many distortions and fabrications about this movement, the movements that emerged after 1975, and more importantly, concerning Islam and the Muslims in general. I have tried to present the subject matter in a manner that was as concise and accurate as possible. To document every single detail of a movement with a history spanning more than 60 years such as the "Nation of Islam" would take volumes and volumes of work.

In a future project, a book entitled *ISLAM AND THE MUSLIMS IN AMERICA.....THEN AND NOW,* Allaah willing, we will attempt to resume where we've left off and also cover and explore some material that we did not cover in the current work. This project will, inshallah, provide a more detailed history of the total picture of Islam in America, and will be a much larger and comprehensive work.

ISLAM IN AMERICA 1995

I have to make one point perfectly clear regarding the book that you've just completed reading: Anything that I've written about any person, past or present, that is deemed negative or controversial, or seems judgmental regarding a certain issue should be viewed as exactly what it is.

It is simply a sincere effort to separate the accurate from the misleading, the fact from the fiction and the myth from reality. Allaah is my witness, what I did not write concerning some of these events, personalities and issues is far worse than what I've presented.

I could have very easily been much more critical and still have been correct both factually and Islamically. As we were editing this book and preparing to go to press, observe for a moment what was printed in a recent edition of the *Final Call,* Louis Farrakhan's newspaper.

In the March 29, 1995 issue, there appears an article on page 29 entitled *THE POWER OF MASTER FARD MUHAMMAD.* In the article, a follower of Farrakhan is recalling a

20 YEARS A.E. (after Elijah)

situation where he was faced with death. The doctors told him that he would not live after being badly burned in a fire.

Read what this misguided, ignorant person said, in the presence of Farrakhan, who is in the photograph that accompanied the article, posing with this man and his wife. This man, who calls himself "Bilal Muhammad" made the following statements:

"I KNOW THAT MASTER FARD MUHAMMAD IS THE TRUE AND LIVING GOD. AND AT THAT MOMENT, AS I WAS DYING, THE FIRST THING THAT CAME TO MY MIND WAS TO CALL ON MASTER FARD MUHAMMAD, BECAUSE HE IS THE TRUE GOD. AND WHEN I CALLED ON HIM, HE ANSWERED. HE SAVED MY LIFE".

If anyone needed further proof as to why I was so adamant about someone giving legitimacy to Louis Farrakhan by calling him a "Muslim leader", this should reaffirm for you how backwards and deviant these people are. **Still, 20 years A.E., people are living the same lie over again and again!**

ISLAM IN AMERICA 1995

So my intention was not to bash or embarrass anyone, or to refute any concepts, ideologies and positions that did not deserve to be refuted. I simply wanted to present enough information, in defense of Islam, to make it very clear what has happened over the past 20 years and prior to that. I want to dispel any confusion that may be present to help those readers who are really seeking the truth. They deserve to know what Islam is and what Islam isn't.

As I said earlier, anything that is found to be factually incorrect, please contact me in writing c/o the publisher. The address is provided at the very beginning of this book. I will respond to your inquiry in writing and try my best to clarify anything that one might not be clear on.

I have also provided a bibliography and a suggested reading list in the back section of the book. This lists reflect nearly all of the books, magazines, journals and periodicals that I read in researching and completing this project. You can also feel free to question me at one of the many lectures and discussions that we plan to conduct regarding this

20 YEARS A.E. (after Elijah)

subject.

Last, but certainly not least, I'd like to thank you, the reader, for patiently reading these words and for supporting this effort at analyzing and examining this very important subject, Islam in America 1995.....20 Years A. E. (after Elijah). I sincerely pray Allaah that He allows each and every person who reads this book to gain some benefit from it, be it big or small.

May Allaah bless all of the Muslims who read this book (and all of the Muslims in general), and may He guide all of the non-Muslims who read this book and are sincerely in search of truth, to accept and embrace Islam, the religion with Allaah, which is based on the Quran and the guidance of Prophet Muhammad ibn Abdullah, the Last Messenger of Allaah, may Allaah's peace be upon him. Allaah has said in the Quran (translated):

"THIS DAY HAVE I PERFECTED YOUR DEEN FOR YOU, COMPLETED MY FAVORS UPON YOU AND HAVE CHOSEN FOR YOU ISLAM AS YOUR DEEN".

ISLAM IN AMERICA 1995

We invite all of the people of America to accept this truth and find the peace, liberation and salvation that you've been searching for.

Anyone that I've wrongfully offended , I offer my sincere apologies, and I ask Allaah, and then you to forgive me. Anyone who I've offended with the truth of Islam, the Quran and the Sunnah, (because after the evidence has been presented and deviation, innovation and falsehood is exposed, you still insist on clinging to some astray concept or ideology) I offer no apologies. But I do ask Allaah's guidance for you.

Surely whatever I have written that is the haqq, the truth, correct, right and exact is from Allaah. And only the mistakes and errors are mine.

20 YEARS A.E. (after Elijah)

BIBLIOGRAPHY

ELIJAH MUHAMMAD

The Supreme Wisdom: Solution to the So Called Negroes Problem.

(Lost-Found Nation of Islam in America, Chicago, IL, 1957)

Message to the Blackman in America.

(Muhammad's Mosque of Islam No. 2, Chicago, IL, 1965)

W. DEEN MOHAMMED

Minister's Kit

(Muhammad's Temple No. 2, Chicago, IL, April 1, 1975-January 1, 1976 [4 Books])

The Teachings of W. D. Muhammad, Book 1; Secondary/Adult Level.

(The Honorable Elijah Muhammad Mosque No. 2, Chicago, IL, 1976)

Lectures of Emam Muhammad.

(W. D. Muhammad Publications, First Edition, Chicago, IL, 1978)

ISLAM IN AMERICA 1995

Religion on the Line.

(W. D. Muhammad Publications, Chicago, IL, 1983)

Imam W. Deen Muhammad Speaks from Harlem, NY Vol. 1.

(W. D. Muhammad Publications, Chicago, IL, 1984)

Imam W. Deen Muhammad Speaks from Harlem, NY- Challenges that Face Man Today- Vol. 2.

(W. D. Muhammad Publications, Chicago, IL, 1985)

An African -American Genesis.

(M.A.C.A. Publication Fund, Calumet City, IL, 1986)

Religion is Sincerity (Pamphlet).

(M.A.C.A. Fund Inc., Calumet City, IL, 1988)

As The Light Shineth From The East.

(W.D.M. Publishing Co., Chicago, IL, 1990)

Al-Islam, Unity and Leadership.

20 YEARS A.E. (after Elijah)

(The Sense Maker, A Muslim Journal Subsidiary, Chicago, IL, 1991)

MUHAMMAD ARMIYA NU'MAN

What Every American Should Know About Islam and the Muslims.

(New Mind Productions, Jersey City, NJ, 1985)

Wisdom From the West.

(New Mind Productions, Jersey City, NJ, 1989)

VARIOUS AUTHORS

STEVEN BARBOZA. *American Jihad: Islam After Malcolm X.*

(Doubleday Publishers, New York, NY, 1994)

C. ERIC LINCOLN. *The Black Muslims in America.*

Third Edition.(Wm. B. Eerdmans Publishing Co., Grand Rapids, MI, and Africa World Press Inc., Trenton, NJ, 1994)

ISLAM IN AMERICA 1995

JOURNAL AND NEWSPAPER ARTICLES

Muhammad Speaks (1963-1975 Issues)

Bilalian News (1975-1981 Issues)

World Muslim News (1981-1982 Issues)

American Muslim Journal (1982-1985 Issues)

Muslim Journal (1985-Present Issues)

All preceding journals and newspapers are published out of Chicago, IL.

M. AMIR ALI. *Islam or Farrakhanism.*

(The Institute of Islamic Information and Education, Chicago, IL, 1991)

The Final Call (1990-1995 Issues) (FCN Publishing, Chicago, IL)

20 YEARS A.E. (after Elijah)

SUGGESTED READING LIST

(This is by no means an exclusive or comprehensive list. It is simply a guide in the right direction in your search to find some of the authentic sources of information about Islam.)

THE NOBLE QUR'AN IN THE ENGLISH LANGUAGE. Translated by Dr. Muhammad Taqi-ud-Din Al Hilali and Dr. Muhammad Muhsin Khan.

(Maktaba Dar-us-Salam, Riyadh Kingdom of Saudi Arabia, Fourth Edition 1994)

SAHIH AL-BUKHARI.

Translated by Dr. Muhammad Muhsin Khan.

(Maktaba Dar-us-Salam, Riyadh Kingdom of Saudi Arabia, 1994)

SAHIH MUSLIM.

Translated by Abdul Hamid Siddiqi.

(Kitab Bhavan, New Delhi, India)

EXPLANATION OF THE CREED.

Imam al-Barbahaaree.

ISLAM IN AMERICA 1995

Translated by Daawood ibn Ronald Burbank.

(Al-Haneef Publicatons, Birmingham, UK, 1995)

THE CALL TO ISLAM AND THE CALLER.

Shaikh `Alee Hasan `Alee `Abdul Hameed.

Translated by Dawood ibn Ronald Burbank.

(Al-Hidaayah Publishing and Dist., Birmingham, UK, 1994)

FUNDAMENTALS OF AQEEDAH AHL-US-SUNNAH.

Jam'iat Ihyaa' Manhaaj Al-Sunnah

(Suffolk, UK, Fourth Print 1993)

TAWHEED AND THE NULLIFICATION OF IMAN AND ISLAM.

Shaikh Muhammad bin Jameel Zeino.

Translated by Abu Khaliyl Al-Ameriyky.

(Da'wa to LA ILLAHA ILLA ALLAH-

20 YEARS A.E. (after Elijah)

MUHAMMAD AR RASOOL ALLAH, Phila, PA)

BLIND FOLLOWING OF THE MADHHABS.

Shaikh al-Ma'soomee al-Khajnadee.

(Al-Hidaayah Publishing and Dist., Birmingham, UK, 1993)

UNDERSTANDING THE EVILS OF INNOVATIONS: BID'AAH.

Jam'iat Ihyaa' Minhaaj-Us-Sunnah

(Suffolk, UK, 1990)

ISLAM IN AMERICA 1995

ABOUT THE AUTHOR

Amin bin Qasim Nathari is a writer and researcher/historian. He specializes primarily in the analysis and documentation of events and issues which impact the Muslims and the Islamic experience in America. He has dedicated himself to providing a correct understanding of Islam and the Muslims both to the media and the general public.

Born in Newark, New Jersey, and currently residing in East Orange, New Jersey, Nathari is a thorough researcher and has developed a solid and respected reputation for his utilization of authentic sources in all of his writings, lectures and presentations.

A frequent lecturer and public speaker, Nathari has traveled extensively throughout the East Coast and has lectured before a wide and diverse range of audiences. Some of the important issues and topics discussed are "Problems and Challenges Facing Muslim Youth", "Islam and the Media", "Adherence to the Sunnah", "Towards Developing an Islamic Infrastructure", and many

20 YEARS A.E. (after Elijah)

others.

Nathari has an extensive record of service within the Muslim community. He is the Executive Director of the Organization of American Muslim Unity (OAMU), a non-profit, community based entity that addresses social, economic and political concerns from an Islamic perspective.

He also serves on the advisory board of the Muslim Family Social Service Center (MFSSC), based in Newark, New Jersey. He is a member of the Muslim Community Development Association (MCDA), based in East Orange, New Jersey, which is currently developing programs to provide an economic base for Muslims within the community which includes establishing the first Muslim credit union in the state of New Jersey.

Nathari is the Managing director of Sabree Communications, a New Jersey based independent media company, actively involved in various aspects of public relations, publishing and audio media communication.

ISLAM IN AMERICA 1995